I LOOKED
in the MIRROR

Her Story

VICTORIA STARR LOVE

I LOOKED
in the MIRROR

Her Story

Empowerment in the Form of Truth to Self
She sees her reflection and finally,
her story is told with the voice of wisdom on her side.

Abuse, Betrayal, & Abandonment to Transformation, Triumph & True Identity

BIG MOOSE
PUBLISHING

© 2025 Victoria Starr Love
Back Cover Author Photo Credit: Mariah Noehl
Cover Art Credit: Mariah Noehl
Published by: Big Moose Publishing
234 Pohorecky Street Saskatoon, SK CANADA S7W 0J3
www.bigmoosepublishing.com

ISBN: 978-1-989840-84-9 (sc)
ISBN: 978-1-989840-85-6 (ebook)

Big Moose Publishing 05/2025

For Michael the Great, Mariah Papaya,
and Little Wolf

My story is your story.
When one awakens, heals and transforms,
a door opens for another to have the same opportunity.
Let it arise and be known.

Forward

This book is a treasure that moves us forward out of the dearth of destruction: our current system. It is an example of the whole person's knowledge. It pushes back against the academy that privileges rigid knowledge production of the mind alone, elevating the knowledge of experience, the body, and the emotions. This unifies us in our whole experience — truly a feminist manifesto at its best.

– Dr. Brenda Anderson, Professor in Women's and Gender Studies
& Religious Studies

My Hope For, You

As you slowly contemplate this book, one chapter at a time, my hope is that each word of poetry, story, and song stirs your heart with great emotion. Healing emerges, transformation occurs, and true identity is revealed when the 'flow of release' is given the grace and freedom to follow its course.

May you be inspired to come alive and feel again, grieve and heal within, dream and become known to you for who you truly are, and see what lives inside your soul. Your miracle begins by embracing pain, facing fears, learning to love, and allowing pleasure to penetrate your very being.

There will be moments in this story where you will question, wonder, and even want to know more; however, this story is meant for you to find yourself in the spaces and places that create questions in your mind and unmask answers for you to discover.

Your interpretation of and kinship with another's story is the beauty that awakens you to your own. May the power of love be with you.

Prologue: *Her Story*

How do you love your story, even when it hurts? What do you do when self-doubt creeps its way into the fabric of your existence and separates you from the beauty of your true identity, worth, and value? *Her story* connects the dots to transformation amid pain and suffering, a *Sacred Journey* of great empathy that sees, feels, and experiences the deepest crucifixions of the heart, healing the unbearable and releasing shame.

When she was a little girl, she was always dreaming. She dreamed she could talk, to have a voice and to be heard. Her dream came from her pain, but her suffering was the very source upon which her gifts and true identity were built. *The Divine Character of Love* blesses her with the gift of visions, apparitions, and dreams that envelop *Higher Wisdom* and reveal secrets to the *Sacred Heart of Truth.* She is given the key to a treasure chest that will open her bosom to a vulnerability so precious that even nature cannot deny its pure existence.

With great courage, she embarks on a path to find the spirit of a girl, intending to connect with the woman she desires to become, all the while surrounded by a storm, a whirlwind of chaos. The demon of loneliness and abandonment came to destroy her. Feeling unloved, she seeks relief from men who abuse her; she is caught in a cycle of trauma, the familiarity of childhood abuse. She has learned to allow the perpetrator, in. Deception, desperation, and disillusionment paint her reality. She must unlearn the lies and transform into the song of joy that she was destined to be and not become paralyzed by the impact of regret and loss. On the contrary, the love of Divine influence is revealed in her relationships with men, causing her to look in the mirror and see clearly.

The erosion of her worth may have begun with a seed of doubt, but a girl with a dream must not die; to the death she was spared, dare to dream. Her transformation begins with remembering. As the veil is lifted from the dark night of her soul, the truth does not bind her; it sets her free. In a vision, she meets a wolf, and he awakens her to the destruction of denial to guide her toward the most powerful instrument in the world — *her* voice.

CONTENTS

Part 3 *Coming Alive*

Part 4 *Here She Is*

"Death is like a mirror in which the true meaning of life is reflected."

– Sogyal Rinpoche

Artwork by Mariah Noehl

Part 1

A Girl, A Woman, and Those Men

To Begin…

Listen to the Music

"Little Wolf," by Karliene. An Arya Stark Fan Song

Chapter One

Spirit of a Girl

A storm drifts in,
and wisdom comes.

Spirit of a Girl

I once knew a girl
I surely did not know
Until that cold and frosty day
Winter

I once felt her grow
I did not know how much
Until that cold and frosty day
Winter

I once dreamt she left
Not knowing why or when
Until that cold and frosty day
Winter

I once heard her scream
I could not see her face
Until that cold and frosty day
Winter

Her Story

Spirit of a Girl

The death of her soul stood still on every street corner, suspended in time like a human corpse in a morgue waiting for its mark of identity, yet lost, without any realization of its existence. There she was — paralyzed. Traumatic memories from her past seemed to follow her wherever she went. It began with the demon of loneliness and the blinding mask of betrayal. As a child, she was abused, abandoned, and taught to tolerate the perpetrator — ignore the signs, stay open, and be silent. Nevertheless, she was determined to find the fingerprint of her identity, the freedom to be delivered from a life of suffering.

Just when she thought peace had entered her path and the chaos had ended, she was tested with fire. The love of her life, her son, was manipulated by his father to leave his mother. He'd soon move two thousand miles away, far off from his family home. What money would she have to see him often? Times were tough. His father's motivation was to eliminate responsibility and obligation. This was a timely move that lessened her ability to protect her family. The ultimate weapon a sick man uses against a mother is her child. And the farther he was away from her, the less he'd have to look at himself. To bend a child's imagination away from a loving parent is an act of violence and hurts a woman at her core.

Nonetheless, the con man had won. She could not believe this was happening to her again. But the men she chose were cold and calculated — familiar. Her spirit was crushed. Her power within weakened. Her identity as a mother withered away. In this time of loss, distant memories flooded her like the constant flow of a river, never-ending. This is the place where remembering began.

Those men.

She has not lost sight of them: the police officers who belittled her for running away from home, yet followed her into back alleys to fondle what they could; the psychiatrist who called her a bitch for voicing the truth about her life at home; the creepy family friend, the doctor, who liked to touch her in places he shouldn't; the opera teacher who stuck his tongue down her throat and caressed her body during singing lessons; the surgeon who did the unmentionable act behind closed curtains; the men who lured her into their cars when she walked home from school; the manager of the restaurant who liked to play touch-me games on music lesson days, while she waited for her siblings and mother to return; the family cult on her daughter's side, who forced her own baby from mother's breast, into an alcoholic home where brainwashing and dependency reaped parental alienation — the grandfather was a crooked cop and forced her into a jail cell at 18 years old, to scare, and alienate her from her own child; the French husband who cheated on her before marriage, leaving her to discover his dishonesty shortly after; the man who almost killed her in the back of a truck — and her father who used anger and rage to justify his hatred. She may not have lost sight of *them*; however, she lost sight of her individuality. They groomed her to believe their sins were hers.

They hurt her. Twisted truth into lies. Stole the girl from her. Silenced the woman.

With guilt and shame, she beat herself up until her mind turned black and blue — as if it all was her fault. Battered with brainwashed thoughts, she sunk into a great depression that led her to realize a black hole lived in her soul. She was terrified to look within and admit the hate they had for her. And now that her son was gone, the last chance of having a *real* family had vanished. In her desperation for a familial bond, she let her guard down.

She had ignored the wisdom of the wolf who came in a

dream to warn her.

In her slumber, as her heavy eyes slept, her spirit was awakened to a naked body. Her almost-to-be corpse lay exposed on the ground of a barren forest, abandoned, near death. The seed of her youth, and the mighty spirit of a woman within, was forced into the paralysis of oppression, and now, she lay vulnerable to the wolf in sheep's clothing.

Moments before her body was fed upon, spirit paralyzed and soul asleep, a white linen cloth came from the sky above and covered her entire body. The wolf moved closer. The silence in the air deafened her. Yet the sound of his coarse fur shook aloud with every step he took, sending a chill down her spine. He came near. His piercing blue eyes met hers with intent. In the same breath, as she gasped for air, fearing attack, the wolf placed his nose in the folds of her most sacred, feminine beauty — a symbolic warning. The strong scent of a woman and her girlish perfume attracted the predator. Nonetheless, she was protected under the *cloth of sanctity.*

The wolf's presence was merely a warning of predator behaviour nearby — a foretelling of the future. But her spirit of strength was made weak by past stories of assault. Although stronger than before and her soul most alive with pure intent, she was vulnerable to violation. In her weakness, she gave in and settled for a lie. Another con man entered her life, promising her the world but leaving her pregnant with regret.

The unhealed child of sorrow grew large inside her abdomen, a sign of continual cycles chasing men who never loved her. The hope was liberation. The repercussion was affliction. Painted on her pretty face was a painful past, blemished with deep-rooted wounds and marked with scars that seeped sadness. She strongly believed that if she gave birth to a child of grief, she would surely die. She was terrified to connect to those scary and suppressed emotions, which were the essence of her true reality. But she had the power to choose between life and death — not only for herself as a woman, but for the one who lived inside of her, the spirit of a girl: alone, afraid, ashamed, and detached. Her swollen womb and the life that now grew within came to remind her that it was time to leave. She needed to let go of her dark, haunting past and follow the light ahead.

On that day of letting go, the wind began to blow, and the sky filled with pure white snow. *Winter* sent a chill down her spine. A cold reminder that if she didn't face her fears, she could end up frozen in time forever. She screamed as she released her past through the delivery of a stillborn child, a real misfortune that was not only traumatic but transformative. In the storm of winter, where a body lay still on the ground of a barren forest, abandoned and near death, the *spirit of a girl* was released — free to find new life. The miracle began with her remembering those cold and frosty days.

And the wolf? He became her best friend, guiding her along the way and telling the tale of wisdom.

Listen to the Music

"O Virtus Sapientiae" Divine Wisdom, Oh Strength of Wisdom, by Hildegard Von Bingen

Chapter 2

Whom Shall I Find?

The heart cannot be
imprisoned
unless the horrors of
darkness put the fire out.

Whom Shall I Find?

Who was I before the knife stabbed at my throat
Ripped at my jugular
Pulled voice out of goat?

Who was I before the prisoners came
Tore heart from broken chest
Pushed soul and spirit to test?

Who was I before the enemies lied
Put up a tall gate
Nailed me like cheap bait?

Who was I before the carousel came
To take me away
From home plate without place?

Who was I, I say!
Who am I, don't you know?
Whisper me something, before I turn cold!

And then it came
One day, before fall
A Messenger's voice
A story for all

"Ashanee you are!
Ashanee my child!
Winter flower so bright!
Flaming fire, ARISE!"

Her spirit was sleeping
To hide from the fright
Her spirit was sleeping
For fear of black night

The devil was lurking
He found a sweet doe
Long strides did he make
To match hooves with her toe

Chameleon's face, did change over time
To make her believe
She was his
And not mine

Confusion and torment
Did harden her eyes
He tried to take over
Still, she surrendered in time

Melted like honey
Dripping sap from cedar tree
Onto earth heartwarming
Bended knee upon knee

"Ashanee you are!
Ashanee my child!
Warrior princess so white
Rose of desert so wild"

"Ashanee you are!
Ashanee my child!
Winter flower so bright
Flame of fire, ARISE!"

(The name Ashanee is of Sanskrit origin, meaning thunderbolt, lightning.)

Her Story

Whom Shall I Find?

The power behind her voice becomes lost in a world built around lies, betrayal, and rage. The spirit of a girl and her emotional flame of fire are forced into a cage of torment. She remains trapped, unable to fly. Innocent, yet imprisoned behind bars. Although unknown to her, the key to her freedom is kept in a treasure chest, and the door of the cage remains open. Despite this, her adult choices produce cyclical outcomes of insanity. She continues to abandon herself.

In the past, she had no choice but to wear heavy chains around her wrists, shackled like a criminal in a prison cell, bound to an environment she had no control over. In the present, she has the power to find the truth amongst the lies that confuse, clarity behind the betrayal that implicates her as the villain, and peace rather than the terror of rage that perpetuates self-abandonment.

Nevertheless, this is all she knows. Repeatedly, she chooses familiar vines that wrap tightly around her neck and choke the breath of life from her very existence. The spirit of destruction, with murderous intent, stabs madly at her jugular, gagging and wounding the true nature of her voice — power, wisdom, truth, and freedom. This is no fault of her own. Learned habits are hard to break.

In her direction, those nearest to her vomit self-hatred, jealousy, and hate, contributing to the disguise she must wear that diminishes her pure beauty. Once painted like a pearl of great price, born with value and worth, her face is now marked with bruises and blood-stained tears. Not a day goes by when she doesn't feel the suffering of her soul. She has carried the wounds of others under her ribs for too long. It's hard for her to let go of the burdens of others while clasping the broken pieces of her own heart.

Her ability to seek freedom is forcibly met with punishment and cruelty; a true enemy nailing her to the burden of another's cross. There appears to be no means to an end, like a carousel spinning around and around without stopping. She never arrives at home plate, where safety dwells. There is only one direction for a ride such as this — stationary. When the voice of a girl is smothered, she feels nothing and becomes despondent. Spiritual growth ceases. She is trapped in the horror of darkness extinguishing her flame of fire, her unique spark. Depression meets her destination — nowhere. She is stuck in the burden of despair.

Looking back, she reflects on her inner child, the confining and domineering spell of human hearts that perpetuated evil — stuck in the terrifying sound of silence. Now, as an adult woman, she has the choice to break free from such grappling hooks. Upon seeing her true identity, she must recollect those cold and frosty days and process her pain for the sake of removing barriers that bind her.

The Master of her destiny, the Divine Character of Love, and Higher Wisdom, bellow out to her, pleading that she see the difference between good and evil so she can rise and connect to her power and true identity within. The voice of her creator calls for her to come back to her true self and visit the place of conscious awareness, the remembering of what is real, what is good, and what is not.

Turning back the pages in time, she recollects a moment in her childhood when her identity became distorted and she disconnected from her true self...

"Stop hurting her! Put her down!" she screamed with conviction at her father. He turned his head to look at her, like in the movie *The Exorcist* when the eyes of the possessed soul meet the onlooker with contempt. Her demand for him to stop only aggravated his hatred and rage. This is where the twisting of truth began: emotional manipulation and psychological warfare.

Spit landed all over her small yet mighty five-year-old face. "How dare you accuse me of such things!" He spewed.

She watched as her sister was lifted off her feet while her father pounded her head into the back door of the house. When she fled to her mother for help, telling her to do something, as she, too, watched closely at the foot of the scene, her mother denied her reality. At that point, logic took over and in her mind's eye, she tried to justify the absurd. "It's not true, what I see, feel, and experience, because *they said so*." On the other side of the coin, her heart said, "Just because your parents don't admit the truth, doesn't mean what *you declare* as truth is wrong." Logic can misconstrue reality. But the heart knows what is real and what is not.

She had wisdom on her side but her family refused to acknowledge this. They were stuck in systems of dysfunction. Unfortunately, this contributed to her wearing a disguise. Her wisdom had to hide. And this is how self-doubt squeezed its way into her world, and she became detached from her true self.

Hiding hinders growth.

As she begins to hear the voice of Spirit, the fear of *black night* vanishes. Evil's deceptive and chameleon-like charm, trying to match his steps with her own, in a long-lived attempt to assault her while trying to hide its own deceptive identity, will soon come to an end. The dark veil inhibiting her vision becomes translucent. The true character of the Divine is becoming more transparent. The hardening of her heart softens, and confusion lifts from her shoulders. The spirit of a girl is now placed within the arms of a woman, where the joining of the two creates wings to fly beyond the bars of imprisonment, far away from the cage of torment. Her eyes are slowly opening to the ever-so-familiar schemes of the perpetrator.

As her emotional fire is lit, the light within her spirit is identified, and transformation begins. She embarks on a new journey to find love and heal her soul. Along the way, she discovers a safe place to lay her sorrow — *on bended knee*. A treasure chest filled with comfort is waiting to hold her heart.

Listen to the Music

"Ov' è, lass', il bel viso?"
From *Madrigali. Six "Fire Songs" on Italian Renaissance Poems*,
by Morten Lauridsen and performed by, Cor Cantiamo

Chapter 3

On Bended Knee

O father protector,
mother of nurture,
surrender to thy daughter,
son and sacred spirit.

On Bended Knee

On bended knee
I lay my chest
Where swollen heart
Finds comfort, rest

Thy hands, they cup
Tears overflow
Beneath your feet
Weep, oh my soul

From bosom beat
Bones broken cold
Burnt embers, ashes
Trials of old

Oh, blessed touch
On forehead feel
Most calm now, peace
Strength to heal

As I arise
Look up and see
Eyes that pierce
Blue light in me

I do now know
On bended knee
There was, will be
You guiding me

I do now know
On bended knee
There was, will be
You with me

Her Story

On Bended Knee

She faces her feelings of deep hurt and sorrow by placing her heart into the hands of a lover, instead of surrendering to the wrath of an enemy. She is ready to begin a new journey, learning to trust herself, heal, and strengthen; and ultimately to love and be loved. She takes one step at a time walking toward the *unfamiliar,* healthier path. She releases tears of sorrow into hands that hold, nurture, remove, and bandage old wounds, drawing her spirit near to a home within her heart that is filled with comfort.

It's time to remove what lay behind, the trauma and trials of old, and walk a new path, one that is light and airy. To do this, she must carve out messages from her mind that brainwashed her to believe she had no worth. Unspoken messages, subtle nuances, and physical actions distorted her image. She came from a family who encouraged *the mean spirit* to control her; this included her siblings, who also learned this behaviour from their parents. The purpose was to use her as a scapegoat, lest she mirror back their dysfunctional patterns. She was to think in the same way as they did, not express her true self, and agree with their thoughts or be met with retribution. Meanness was seen as tolerable and normal. Individuality, difference, and unique personalities adding variety to society, were not encouraged.

But she was not going to allow this mind control. In her heart, she knew it was wrong because it made her feel sick to her stomach. She needed a guiding and blessed touch to bring her strength to heal. An embrace like this would warm her heart and unite her with her dreamer's imagination — one of self-expression, sparked by an internal dialogue that affirmed her direction.

As she arises from a trauma state, disconnected from her

unique identity, and looks up to something beyond suffering, her soul begins to enlighten. Her eyes become pierced by an angelic blue light, illuminated by a Higher Power. She is reunited with Wisdom. She becomes aware of the one who *is* and *has been* guiding her all along. In this awestruck moment, she connects the dots to a Sacred Spirit and the brow of her humanness.

Trust begins. Trust takes time. Trust is the key to opening her treasure chest.

She embarks on this newfound journey, ascertained by baring her soul on the bended knee of *The Sacred Spirit of Love,* who offers loving hands in return for tears. This Spirit is symbolic of a father protector and a mother who nurtures; they hold a safe space for the expression and acceptance of a child's wisdom and identity. When care is given, the spirit of a girl can be guided home, where the heart is. This exchange is a life-giving force that empowers and prepares her to arise and become known to the call of her heart, the true character of her existence.

The love she experiences on the bent knee of The Sacred Spirit of Love is like a white veil of protection that is hardly noticeable by sight. It's a faint whisper, a breath sweeping against her face, like soft bristles touching the canvas ever so gently, reminding her that she will be nurtured along the way. With a sigh of relief in this newfound relationship, she presents her deep-rooted pain as a gift offered into the hands of compassion.

On bended knee, love guides her to see and accept herself as she is, a *song of joy.*

Listen to the Music

"Gabriel's Oboe — for Cello & Orchestra," by Ennio Morricone.

Chapter 4

Carry Me

Inner strength full of song,
sing to me my identity!

Carry Me

I wanted a man to carry me
For a very, very long time

I needed a man to carry me
For a very, very long time

I hoped and prayed for a man to carry me
For a very, very long time

Alas…

I ascertained, that music carried me
And so, I became a song

I found pleasure in the goddess of her treble clefs
Bass clefs took me deep within

High notes brought heaven to my dreams
Low notes balanced my reality

Dancing to staccato was like magic
Long notes sanctified me with truth

Half notes taught me to let go
Whole notes gave me hope

Rests brought a breath of freedom
Signature time was set for me

What I most wanted was…

My heart to carry me
For a very, very long time

My mind to carry me
For a very, very long time

My spirit to carry me
For a very, very long time

Now, I carry me

Her Story
Carry Me

The power that is created in a loving partnership with yourself composes a sweet melody of joy! Love like this should never be minimized. LOVE is POWERFUL! It provides strength, inspiration, and motivation.

Amid family dysfunction, her mother gave her the gift of music. Monday music lessons were the cat's meow for getting out of school early. From the age of four, she studied violin and piano. At twelve, she became bored with learning the music of others and began composing songs on the piano. But she wanted something different: to study voice. In the same year of her boredom, she began taking singing lessons with an opera singer. She had a strong desire to express the voice of an angel that was inside of her. When she sang, she connected to her authentic self. She was excited to embark on a lifelong vocal journey. In her adolescence, this was one of the most, sincere decisions she had ever made for herself.

Sincere love and the connection with *the self,* bring one to the highest of all heights. Absence does not make the heart grow fonder, or even stronger, for that matter. An intimate knowingness and communion with herself promote good health and increase her confidence. It builds a strong connection between your heart and your head, creating clarity. It provides mental, emotional, spiritual, and physical human growth. The exchange of sincere, true, and intimate love is strength-building in a mutually reciprocated relationship, but most importantly, it must first begin with her.

The trouble began when she sought to find love from a man to fill a void in her heart that was created in childhood. Attempting to heal *the wound of absenc*e by expecting a man, or anyone else, to bandage another's sorrow will only end with disappointment. Filling a void like this begins with self-reflection, awareness, doctoring the pain, and attending to the loss endured during childhood.

When the right kind of love is *not* given at a young age, a hole in the soul develops and creates a space that is open to violation. It must be filled with goodness, mended with compassion, and healed with care to protect it. Ultimately, this is a choice to be practiced by the wounded adult. In the poem Carry Me, *she* must pursue her authentic self and build her identity to become whole.

Choosing to take her musical endeavours in the direction of singing was one of the first decisions she made that connected her to her authentic self. Yet this decision, through no fault of her own, led to sexual abuse. Her opera teacher began fondling her. He would make her stand in front of a mirror and tell her how pretty she was, touch her breasts, stroke her stomach, and slide his large hands across her face. Once, he forced his mouth on hers and stuck his tongue down her throat while at the same time fondling her naked breasts under her blouse.

She loved to sing, but anger got the best of her. It became her protective armour, but it also caused her to remain stuck in trauma because she never knew how to get rid of it. She thought telling on him would help. She told her mother about what he was doing, and her reality was denied. Shortly after this, she ran into her opera teacher in the lobby of the Conservatory of Music. Just the scummy look on his face triggered her. She lashed out at him with anger and confronted him about his unethical behaviour. But she was met with extreme rage and gaslighting. She wasn't scared of his anger. She was terrified of being denied her truth. Self-doubt made her mind and heart sick.

Her mother's lack of acknowledgment and the terror she felt because of his denial caused her to leave music altogether. Could it have been different if her mother had acknowledged his abuse? And why would her father and mother defend him in court even though seven other women made allegations against him?

What were they protecting?

An open door of *non-protection* caused her to believe that it was acceptable for others to violate her. It was normalized behaviour and sketched onto her face, marking her with a *look of availability* for predators to devour. She was framed to be open and programmed to believe that wickedness is admissible.

There were times when she'd walk home from school, and older men would pick her up in their car, take her to their homes and sexually abuse her. She was paralyzed and disillusioned by what she was previously taught: stay silent, ignore your truth, and be open to wicked ways. *What you see and experience is not real.* Her parents' friend, a doctor, loved to come and visit when she was sick and inappropriately examined her. Even before the opera singer, she remembers being left at restaurants with male managers who would take her to their apartments and entice her with alcohol so they could get into her pants. She told her parents. But when she did, it became a crazy-making mind affair. Her father would gaslight her by stating, "How can you do this to me?" And her mother continued to deny her reality — an often, repeated pattern in childhood. They would say, "This is *just* what she does." She was groomed to tolerate and allow the predator in.

The loss of parental protection provokes and paves an undeniable path for a child to behave in dysfunctional ways. Abandonment has detrimental and life-altering effects. Extreme behaviour is the result. A child accepts and gravitates toward familiar patterns of behaviour, an attempt to have foundational needs met. This becomes a habit in adulthood, seeking that which attempts to meet a need but is dysfunctional. As an adult, she functioned in a state of desperation and became attracted to the only thing she knew — *danger.* She was easily convinced by the con man that he was *good.* However, the pain experienced while reflecting on these memories motivates her to take another road toward fulfillment.

It begins with her.

She changes her tune. She seeks to find musical notes that live inside her goddess nature and encapsulate more of her authentic self. To sing a new song, she must write a new melody. She traces lines back to her youth; in much the same way circular rings on the inside of a tree represent a year of life, each carrying a story, she begins to revisit and rewrite her future. Her story must be seen for what it is: a cycle of engaging in patterns of behaviour that perpetuate her past: loneliness, abuse, abandonment, and betrayal. It is time to build a whole new world.

Acknowledgment will create the shift she deserves. She can change.

What she seeks to find in a man to fulfill her heart's destiny, she must discover in herself as a woman. Every woman needs a song in her heart that is created from her very own existence. She begins to discern that looking, hoping, and praying for a man to carry her will never entirely satisfy her soul. The personality of a *misogynist* is one she must understand better so she can protect herself as time moves on.

The tight vice grip of domination and control that was used to suppress her inner power became her provocation to find and connect to a deeper place within, where freedom was her bottom line. She WILL reclaim her power. By recognizing her song within, the source that inspires her to create her magic, she begins to renew her mind and remove records from the past. The best medicine to bring transformation is for her to fall in love with her story.

Emotions rise and fall. New melodies lift her to foreign places.

Her expression of sensuality and how she displays her feminine beauty are adored. Pleasure brings enjoyment without guilt. She determines her worth and value. Like a small child discovering the world for the first time, she explores a new reality: love in the form of truth to self. She learns that she can carry herself. In the same measure, she must not forget to protect what has been found. She must listen to her heart above all else when logic doesn't tell the whole story.

There are those who, even when faced with death, refuse to look in the mirror. They inflict piercing wounds upon society, sucking the life out of humanity. On her journey towards freedom, she comes across a man who tries to appear loving and tricks people into believing his intentions are good. He is self-serving. On his deathbed, she listens to his last words that reap the anguish of misery. In its truest form, she sees more clearly the factors underlying the behaviour of a predator. She must take this lesson in observation and apply it to her future. Her power within is the connection and acceptance of her sight, senses, and sensibility.

A man with no sense of moral identity is dangerous.

Listen to the Music

"Listen," by Beyoncé

Chapter 5

Personal Private Sufferings

The root of all evil
begins with a thought of
inadequacy, then a mad
search for self-worth in a
pool of materialism, wealth,
power, and domination.

Personal Private Sufferings

What kind of man am I
Who owns the riches of the world
Wealth beyond character
Power perpetuating unholy pleasure?

My indulgence in materialism
Brings others to eat scraps from darkened streets
Beg mercy for winning wealth
Hospitalizing the insecure, diagnosing insanity

I voice that privacy is perfect
Yet, secrets hide the truth
With dark veil and destruction
Mangling the mouths of babes, killing opportunity
For sweet youth

I swim in a virus
Spitting breath like a whirlwind
Raining on heads maddening with aggression
Insecurity lurks with disease and paralysis

Oh, how Great Thou Art
For dollars rule, not sense
Gold melts like an antidote
One more dose sustains me

My thoughts are like murder
Moments of bliss do not last
Looking at the seduction of my secrecy
I ask, who am I?

Her Story

Personal Private Sufferings

In the life of a man who breeds capitalism and riches beyond sufficiency, humankind suffers. It is here that an older man, nearing the end of his life, looks back and sees the atrocity of his greed. He becomes aware of how he played a part in widening the gap between the rich and the poor and dominating others with abuse and control. His attitude of superiority is a stench that has made even him sick. Up until this point, he has been regrettably indifferent about the magnitude of his destructive choices.

He chose to walk by and ignore the homeless suffering on the street, frown upon them with contempt for their weakness, instead of offering grace and humility. Rather than place a penny in their pockets, bringing a small amount of hope for relief, he ignores the problem of poverty, as if it were nonexistent. He prefers to rest in the comfort of his penthouse, built high upon the rocks of a poor country, and look down at his hired slaves as they toil and sweat endlessly in a cycle of false hope.

He has turned a blind eye to his ability to provide security for future generations. Requests for financial aid during emergencies are denied, leaving those less fortunate helpless and hopeless. Humanity is forced to crawl deep into its black hole of despair; unresolved shame due to impoverished conditions creates poor mental health, yet *they* are diagnosed as insane.

Meanwhile, he makes deals to grow his ego bigger than the sum of his true worth. He is addicted to the *high* he gets from holding great wealth and power, perpetuating an endless cost to those who can never attain it under his regime. He has risen to the top at the expense of losing friends to anger, workers to death, and families to division. He has been unable to self-reflect on how his behaviour negatively impacts the lives of others.

He secretly cons anyone who crosses his path by putting dollars into his pockets, while at the same time, making no sense to others or society. His narcissism revealed a merciless and unempathetic character, muffling the voice of wisdom from a youthful generation crippled by his mistakes.

As society becomes increasingly sick because of his greed, he works hard to hide the secret of his wealth: self-indulgence. Because of this, he wears a mask to hide from *his dark veil* and destruction. Attaining gold in exchange for money has been the only antidote to keep addictive, murderous thoughts away from feelings of inferiority and insecurity. Dose after dose, dollar after dollar, keeps him from feeling his lack of materialized identity, and his low self-worth.

On his death bed, as he breathes his last breath, he is awakened by the realization that his soul contains a black hole. It is open and exposed. Empty and barren. And there is no time left to fill it. He lacks the true kingdom of success: love, care, and compassion. He is alone. No one sits by his side.

As his eyes get heavy and his heart slows, he begins to see how his seductive existence brought sickness and disease, not only to himself but to humanity. Black-hole predators create black-hole victims. Now that he cannot escape death, with no one by his side to bring him comfort, grief overwhelms his heart, and a question arises in his mind. "Who am I?" He dies in a state of paralysis, unable to look in a mirror.

It is this kind of man who stole her heart time and time again — the black-holed soul. They don't change. She needs to. Listening to his confession, hearing him cry out for help as he questions his ways, awakens her to what could happen if she keeps choosing the familiar. She must not waste her life in another's cage or live desperate and vulnerable behind another's prison wall.

What a tragedy! To die not knowing thyself! The admission from this man on his deathbed propels her forward to find her own identity and secure her future. The perpetrator cannot be tamed; therefore, self-protection must be learned. Instead of begging for love from men like this, who can never give her what she needs, she takes another step forward on the path toward finding her true identity.

Listen to the Music

"They Don't Really Care About Us," Brazil version, by Michael Jackson

Chapter 6

Wasted Breath

Beggars choose their poison
and drink its venom.

Wasted Breath

Why beg for love if it chooses *not*, come near
How could a soul even bear such a burden be
I would rather die, have wasted breath
come close or nearest me

Its poison is no less than deadly venom
Trickling down my spine, no time for a plea
Unlocks the clock strikes death or two
Before due time, no chance to flee

Worthiness whilst trying to prove
Returns no kiss, lacks touch and care
Removes reality, a mask in place
Crazy-making mind affair

Do not dare, not even try
To ask for what is not inside
The heart of a man, the voice of a woman
For all will forever deny, deny, deny

Her Story

Wasted Breath

Begging for love is similar to believing that water can be squeezed out of a stone. It's insanity. Begging is a dead-end act. It's like being buried alive in a hole, suffocating to death with eyes wide open, awake while losing breath. She recognizes an inescapable suffering of its kind, which festers a type of madness, producing holes in her heart. For this reason, she must stop chasing *fabricated love.*

Nevertheless, her inner strength, wisdom, and intuition are heightened. She can let go of carrying an addictive burden, which the chase brings. She wastes not one more breath pursuing a relationship with someone who could never love her the way she needs to be loved.

At this pivotal point in her life, she decides to let go of trying to prove herself worthy of love, for she knows that if she continues in this way, she will soon be poisoned by paralysis. The death of her soul will arrive before due time. Absolute exhaustion will bring her body to a state of sickness and disease. Trying to prove herself worthy when love would rather not come near brings disappointment and heartache. So, she attempts to stop *the cycle of insanity.* She is stronger and wiser than before. She refuses to partner with a crazy-making mind affair. The lesson she learns, she shares with all of humanity.

"Do not waste your breath pursuing love when it would rather not come near. Imaginary love is not worth it. Do not ask for what will forever be denied!"

To beg for love when it never existed in the first place is death to the soul. Life begins when the cycle of insanity is broken and new seeds are planted, bringing forth life instead of death.

Listen to the Music

"No Love," by Noak Hellsing

Chapter 7

Precious Petals

Age is the presence of today, not the withering away of the body near death or the timeless spirit that lives on.

Precious Petals

What is age
when your beauty
speaks sweet youth?

And by grace, your love is revealed like a freshly picked flower
its unique scent awakens young love
like a colourful bouquet...

Innocence, purity, excitement and adulation
something never before touched, until now
For the first time...

It is you who waters my garden and gives life to a thirsty rose
it is I who drinks from the pollen
of your passionate soul

Embracing the seed of your love
planted and blooming deep within my heart
remembering, today is the present and tomorrow is unknown

So, for now
I will bathe in the essence
Of your most beautiful, precious petals

Her Story

Precious Petals

Although time has passed, hard lessons have been learned, and scars remain in sight inner beauty never ages. It's timeless. The Universe sends her a message of hope, to meet *self-worth* in the palm, held wide open, of an older man — an affirmation of freedom for her to fly high like a bird, be all she can be, and become all she is. He is twenty-seven years older. A European romantic. She is Danish and Swiss. A similar connection based on descent gives her wings to fly. Love unexpectedly blesses her.

As she continues to turn away from a lifelong cycle of insanity, chaos meets calm. His wisdom and affection arrive just in time for her to find out what security feels like and the grounding effect it has. To know her worth secures her future. With a gentle touch, he affirms her worth and value. Confidence within her grows. She opens up like a flower and makes herself vulnerable to his tender and thoughtful care.

She falls in love with him.

She discovers the beauty that lives in the essence of her spirit and embraces the sweetness that awakens her, a little bit more, to who she is. A dying and thirsty rose she once was, now drunk on the passionate soul of her lover. Before she met him, she did not connect to her worth or understand what it meant; with him, she learned to plant new seeds: self-love, self-care, and self-adoration. Transformative actions attract *seeds of real love.*

His sincerity of heart blooms within her own, growing roots that heal deep wounds of loneliness and low self-worth. He mirrors her, a reflection of who she is. A rose worthy of protection. He writes her letters, telling her what he sees. Paints her pictures of dragonflies, representing her ability to transform. He listens quietly, giving her a voice to express, and touches tenderly, holding her heart next to his with care. This naturally allows her to open her heart so she can see her true worth and intrinsic value. She gains *heart sight.* Vulnerability and surrendering to her delicate nature become her strength. His love, even though his age is beyond hers, brings sweet youth, like a freshly picked flower that, with memory, never dies.

Today, she embraces his love, for her intuition tells her that tomorrow will bring an ending to a relationship that was not meant to last forever. She will miss him, but she has to learn what it is like to miss herself and then embrace the glory of finding her face of identity. So, for now, she will bathe in the essence of his most beautiful, precious petals and embrace a gift that will last a lifetime. She discerns and begins to remember that goodness and love, the true character of Higher Wisdom, can be hers. But will she find another lover of her own?

Listen to the Music

"A Time For Us," by Nina Rota, from the 1968 film
Romeo and Juliet

Chapter 8

Timeless Wonder

The force of penetration is
ecstasy, bliss, life!

Timeless Wonder

A Hindu God's presence
never fades over time
His sentiment, masculinity
absorbs her every second of the clock
turning her towards Him

He fulfills a sensuous dream
a world where fanaticism and romance
is met by poetic thought
and bigness of mind

His power persuades her
she surrenders to his chest
enters onto lap
where lovemaking is the ultimate flight

He penetrates her with His goodness
she warms like a red apple
becoming ripe in the heat of the sun
dangling on the tip of branch
ready to gravitate to earth

Yet instead, falls into His hand
for Him to enjoy the bliss of her fruit
He rolls her in His palm
feeling every curve, smooth bottom
and stem of life

Biting into bare skin
she squeals with pleasure
as the fruit of her loin
runs down
His face and into His mouth

Heaven becomes her
Paradise is His
the hands of time
are forever theirs

Her Story

Timeless Wonder

Her lover, who brought many lessons, leaves. Her heart aches for some time, but she continues to experience goodness and love as she moves onward. Pleasure was not something she was allowed to experience growing up. It was considered a sin, vanity. Demonized. Narcissists can't feel true pleasure and so they will hate you for feeling your own. Happiness and laughter were scorned, and to enjoy life was considered shameful. Play and the enjoyment of self was shunned. In recompense for this distortion of reality, she is touched by another aspect of love — a blissful, intimate penetration of ecstasy. Communing with the Master of her destiny surpasses earthly understanding.

To her, this is a reminder of the nature of God as she envisions a Higher Power to be — a lover in pursuit of her heart, igniting a passion to enjoy life and to be enjoyed. He never leaves her side. He adores her and everything about her. He wants to be near her. And this makes her feel important. His expressive, masculine sentiment absorbs her every second of the day, building trust that turns her always in his direction.

Together, they lean into a world where their intelligence becomes one, bringing similar dreams of fantasy and a poetic story about a life worth living! They are each other's equal, joining forces above earthly conditions. The persuasive power of this union has her leaning into Him. Her racing heart and His pounding chest draw her close to Him. She opens as if she's been given a safe place to dwell. She surrenders to the entryway of partnership, lathering him with female goodness, soaring gracefully towards an ultimate flight of making sweet, sweet love. The making of love represents the forming of identity and self-expression. He gives to her, and she gives to Him. He penetrates her with His goodness, warming her face like a red apple, ripening her fruit in the heat of the sun.

She drifts towards heaven as bliss enters her spirit. Daring to dangle on the edge of the unknown, the tip of a branch where love appears to be dangerous. He holds her tight, showing commitment, unearthing her uncertainty, so she can feel what is real. She attempts to gravitate down to earth and instead falls into His hand.

To her surprise and with a sense of relief, he enjoys the bliss of her fruit. He rolls her in the palm of His hand, enthusiastically studying and learning each mark of her pure beauty. He feels her every curve, smooth bottom, and stem of life and reveals to her what a magnificent masterpiece she is. Art made in the name of love. He cannot stop exploring! He enjoys the creation of His hands and experiences great pleasure. A reciprocal exchange made known to each other! To be known... a mystery worth unravelling!

With His mouth wide open, where knowledge and discovery begin, the fruit of her loin runs down His face and into His mouth. He tastes the sweetness of her being, her humanness, coming to a place of understanding of her, and in return, affirms the purity in pleasantry. *Paradise is His and Heaven becomes her*. The hands of time are forever theirs. Lost in a moment in time, they share a moment of bliss, intimacy, and ecstasy. They become known to each other. To be known is the ultimate flight of humanness.

Her discovery of His delight in her, and hers in Him, gives her hope and wisdom to move beyond a stagnant and ordinary life and instead be enjoyed for who she is, embracing the pleasure that comes her way. This relationship cannot be lost. This relationship always was. It is infinite. In this present moment, the penetration of intimate love and the purity in pleasantry will never again be demonized.

Listen to the Music

"Nearer, My God to Thee: A cappella," by Eclipse 6,
featuring Madilyn Page

Chapter 9

Infinite Love

Not even the power of the Universe can keep stars from falling into the atmosphere. Still, in all its darkness, the black sky of night cannot touch us.

Infinite Love

When I love you, you love me, in return
we float up to the Universe
towards infinite Space
as one

Harmony between us
is masterful
our angels and demons
perfectly aligned

Love
feeling this Higher Power
brings us closer to perfection
human limits disappear

So close we are
even in the distance
soon, our eyes will meet
and stars will fall

Her Story

Infinite Love

As she experiences Higher Wisdom along the way, her inner confidence skyrockets beyond self-defeating limitations. Her vibrant and energetic aura of soft yellows, pinks, and oranges exudes from her! She smiles more and shines like a bright star in a dark sky. So, this is a joy! The Cosmos loves her right back by embracing her true nature. This connection of oneness holding infinite possibilities is a delight. She begins to seek enjoyment instead of just cowering in the face of survival. The possibility is found when two sides of the world are experienced. How can we know what brings pleasure if pain isn't experienced? What motivation would there otherwise be to make a decision when a crossroad presented itself?

Harmony and balance are mastered when perfection and imperfection are seen as natural parts of human life. *Angels and demons become perfectly aligned.* Two opposites reveal pure representations of each other. The contrast between light and darkness is inevitable. She needed to see both sides, the extremes, the good and the bad, to fully embrace infinite love. The ability to see one side creates the ability to see the other. This is called *soul alignment.* Soul alignment can be described as *infinite love*, the highest of all knowledge coming together, revealing the ability to dissolve human limits, thus bringing everything into a state of absolute being.

This absolute place of being represents a spiritual awakening, a renewed sense of understanding, and a love connection with the greater Universe. She embraces the vast distance between the mysteries of life and, in contrast, revelation. In her heart, she carries a knowingness that consciousness will be seen and revealed at the right time. Like a bright falling star that leaves a streak of light across the night sky, she anticipates transformation amid the unknown.

The deep connection she receives from the Universe, alongside her increasing confidence, brings her to meet the *eye of the infinite* in all its vastness and luminescent culmination. To be certain and uncertain, to know but not know everything, this is the magic in the mystery of life.

Listen to the Music

"Le grand cahier: IV. Nos études," by Alexander Litvinovsky

Chapter 10

Then Came Jupiter

What separates the heart
from the head is a faraway
planet, a gravitational
pull towards uncertainty,
creating distance from self.

Then Came Jupiter

Just when I thought
you were untouchable, or
I was just a round, ball of denial
searching for the impossible

There you were…

Out of nowhere
you appeared
with heart wide open
words tender and sweet
actions most complete

You called me on the phone
to brighten my day
you caressed my sorrows
and sadness away

You brought me gifts
of homemade fashion
sparking desire
to express my passion

You pressed your thoughts
deep inside mine
intense, connection
time after time

After…

Talking and teasing
bonding and breaking
feeling and fighting

Then came Jupiter (uncertainty)

Her Story

Then Came Jupiter

He offers sentiments that are slowly becoming familiar to her: acceptance and safety. He awakens her to the true meaning of *bonding*. Bonding occurs when a safe place is created to express innate emotions and fleeting feelings, and at the same time, to have those emotions and feelings responded to. The only other time she truly felt she offered this experience of bonding to another human being was with her son. When he was born and his small body was placed on her bosom, a crying child was calmed by a caring touch, removing the fear of the unknown and anxiety of separation. He felt safe, secure, and accepted. His vulnerability was reciprocated with love. He melted into her life, and a bond was created.

There is something very special to be said about birth and bonding. The bond of *firsts* is an adhesive glue that when threatened or intruded upon, creates a sense of fear, anxiety, loss of power, rejection, and hopelessness, in the same way her bond with her mother was interrupted and her father-daughter relationship was not created. So, for her to feel this shared and adhesive communion, to openly express feelings and emotions, is invigorating! She can begin to relax through self-expressing and mirroring.

This is unlike past experiences, where pain separated her head from her heart, and self-differentiation was intolerable — a scary place to be. But she soon discovers a new presence: the expansive space to express emotions and feelings that lift her out of this world! Her conscience is elevated, and she opens her heart just a little bit more towards vulnerability expression and the actualization of unconditional love. She meets her superhero and thinks he will save the day, and he does, momentarily. But this is just the beginning.

What is believed to be *untouchable*, like a planet suspended in space, is now tangible and present. In the form of old-fashioned love gestures, this man creates a place where unconditional love is generously given and openly received. Surrounded by the light of this presence, she gravitates upward towards Jupiter, a place of uncertainty, where she can feel safe.

In this experience, she is no longer bound by a gravitational pull downward. She bonds with the unknown and is lifted up! This is a positive movement. She becomes present with her emotions and feelings, and even though they appear scary at first, she can discover more of herself in a safe place. While bonding in this relationship, she embarks on a new path that affirms meaning and purpose: deep conversations, shedding tears of humour fighting fair, and exchanging views become a discovered expression of her human experience. WOW! Is this what it's like to feel human? What a superpower!

Her heart is wide open to this moment. The round ball of denial that used to spin out of control, creating a cycle of anxiety and fear, stops. Instead, she partners with unconditional love, a bond that secures confidence even in the unknown. Uncertainty becomes her friend. Rather than living an independent life, once glorified in childhood, she discovers an essential aspect about self-discovery: the need for bonding and how human connection creates a calm in the midst of the unknown. A new light shines her way. The dark sky of depression lifts. Soaring upward, she gradually meets transformation.

Just when she thought the terror of fear, separation, and anxiety would take her down, then comes Jupiter, the planet of *uncertainty*, revealing the magic in its mystery. With this valid lesson in mind, she soon discovers she doesn't need a man-hero to be completely whole. Yes, bonding is a prerequisite for a healthy relationship, but she also needs to learn how to have a relationship with herself and become her superhero!

Goodbye man-hero! Hello, inner strength!

Listen to the Music

"Theme from *Superman*," by John Williams

Chapter 11

Beauty and the Beast, We Are

Find me as I am, and I will become known.

Beauty and the Beast, We Are

You call me Beauty
You say you're the Beast
Beauty and the Beast, *we* are

I as *Beauty*

For when you say, "You are beautiful!"
I feel as though I could conquer the world
Love without fear
Give without strings attached
Be transparent — fully human

You as *Beast*

For you have a gift, I see
Strong emotions ignite a world of change
Love protects at all cost
Giving is from your heart
Sentimental transparency — superhuman

Wisdom connects Beauty to the Beast…

You are also *Beauty*

Your touch is gentle and kind
Silliness shines on your face with patience
Caring for others is pure intent
Eyes, ice blue, search for me
Hair of length, distinguished — royally handsome

I am also a *Beast*

I have a fire within, burns bright red hot
Voice, ferocious, advocate for justice
Brave, not afraid to confront, take charge
Stand up against the odds, fight for what is right
Hair of length, flowing — queen Rapunzel at best

I am Beauty, you are Beast.
You are Beauty, I am Beast.
Beauty and the Beast, *We Are*.

Her Story

Beauty and the Beast, We Are

Coco Chanel once said, "Beauty begins the moment you decide to be yourself." For her to truly be who she is, she must accept attributes of her identity that are unknown to her. She must see masculine characteristics of strength and, at the same time, surrender to her wispy feminine nature, laced with a gown of silk, transparent, yet finely knit together.

To help her along the way, a beast enters her path. She is blown away by their similarities, yet they are also different. Beauty is needed to balance the nature of the Beast, and the Beast is needed to protect her against human nature's way of beating down *pure* Beauty.

She falls in love with one she first sees as her opposite: a voice of mighty thunder, dark eyes that strike far into man, and long locks of silver, tangled hair, unkept to the eye, yet intriguing. One would gasp upon a single gaze, but to her, he is glorious! From the outside, he looks rough, tough, and weird. He is perceived by others as unpleasant, fierce, and dangerous. But to her, he represents protection.

She imagines having that same fierceness as a child. Maybe it could have protected her. But imagining what lies behind, as if the past had been different, will not propel her forward; therefore, she wants to attain the lion within and protect her future. She has longed to feel the grain of tough and protective skin around her soul, a sense of safety, like armour repelling the fiery darts of insecurity. There is no better time than now to join the circle of life and merge the creator's inventorship of mirroring polarity.

What she doesn't realize is that she's had a fighter spirit within her all along. She's been a threat to those who refuse her truth, is looked upon unpleasantly by those who feel inferior to her and is feared by the dark side of the world. In time, she'll fully realize the potential of her warrior spirit within, her lioness. At the same time, there is another side to the Beast: tenderness. This quality is equally important to her. What lies hidden beneath his brow, in the depth of his soul, is the expression of bold empathy.

Her nurturing soul exposes the Beast's tenderness; she teaches him to look at the tough side of his personality — a shield that has hindered others from getting close to him. He had not fully understood how his unresolved pain and resentment made him an angry man, causing others to stay clear of his misery. He had taken a protective disposition to the extreme and used it against himself. The Beauty's presence brings balance and harmony to a rugged soul.

Nonetheless, she is in awe of him because he sees and acknowledges her true beauty. From this, she learns to emphasize her own. As they dance a tangled exchange, they learn a great deal about themselves. They are awakened to a love that is deeper than meets the eye, a *love that reveals the best and the worst in human nature*. Wisdom teaches, that when two opposites collide, one world becomes known. When tough meets tender and tender meets tough, awareness is heightened.

Beauty and the Beast see and accept each other for who they truly are. What first appears to be different brings a reflection of individuality. She sees and admires his strength and finds a way to connect to her own. He sees her tenderness and believes it's safe to express his own. The miracle of unity ascending between them, despite what appears to be different, makes clear the truth of themselves.

When he calls her *Beauty*, he mirrors her strength. When she says, *I love you*, tenderness becomes him. The Beast, in his fierceness, is tamed. Beauty, in her tenderness, becomes wild. Beauty and the Beast, *they are*.

Listen to the Music

"Celtic Dance: A cappella," by Kirby Shaw, featuring SATB Choir

Chapter 12

A Million Years

The beauty of the
unfamiliar becomes known
to those who see.

A Million Years

Two different worlds, one moment in time
once, thousands of miles apart
now, on my doorstep, you have arrived

Your existence I never knew until this present moment
but in spirit, it is as if
I have known you for a million years, before

For the first time
you lay open your chest in trust to my heart
the soul inside you reminded me of mine

And I remembered…

Once, without blemish, released just to be me
to dream, to love, to cry, to see
all that I needed, to be utterly free

At a time when I thought I would never return
from the distance separating my heart in two
far, far away from the magical world within

There you were, in your presence
so real, still-timeless life
those thousands of miles away, those millions of years ago

Here, once two oceans away
I remember
Who I am

Her Story

A Million Years

As she continues on this spiritual journey of remembering and becoming, she strives to remove character flaws — the beliefs of those who rejected her. Still, she has much to learn. One man alone cannot give her everything she needs to look honestly at herself in the mirror. She must face deep-rooted fears of abandonment. Was she ever wanted? This question in her mind is terrifying to think about! She'll need to slowly take one step at a time to build inner strength. At least now, she knows it's in her.

As she sits in her car, daydreaming, with the door wide open, long blonde hair blowing in the wind, like vines reaching up to the heavens, a passerby catches sight of her. She notices him. She delights in his chocolate-butter skin all wrapped up in handsome, and her fair complexion draws him in. He is not from around here. He came from another country, a great distance away. To her surprise, he approaches her and looks ocean-deep into her eyes.

She shivers in his presence at the realization of how unique they are, like two different worlds, one moment in time colliding. She's not going to let this moment slip away. Her inner compass tells her to let him in. At first sight, she remembers something about herself that was lost a long time ago. She can't quite explain it or even understand what she's seeing in her mind's eye. But she can feel its pull. Once thousands of miles apart, now, on her doorstep, something foreign yet beautifully familiar arrives. His presence feels new to her; on the other hand, she senses something inside his spirit that reunites her with a part of herself that she lost a million years ago. She's remembering. Whatever was lost has arrived.

They walk, talk, and embrace. She feels the heaviness in her heart lighten. As he lays his head on her chest, he tells her she has a *big mind*. "You see beyond the human mind and into the heart of the Creator."

Before falling into the hands of abusers, she was blemish-free, a timeless light source, pure and filled with joy. She carried hope and freedom that radiated like sunbeams warming the earth and grounding her presence. She was able to dream without restrictions, love without limitations, and cry without shame. She saw things for how they were. *She was wanted.* And she knew it. This gave her wings to fly into a world of wonder — as she was. In this predestined moment, she follows her heart's sight. She accepts herself as wanted — with a big mind and not like the others.

Painful scars from the past begin to fade. Before, they represented the distance between herself and the spirit of love and now, she feels a rekindling connection that reunites her with a higher intelligence and her true identity. At a time when she thought she'd never return from the distance that separated her heart in two, from a faraway world within, there he was. The presence of this man, in this ever-so-real moment, represents a timeless life of hers that never left.

She had just forgotten.

That which had been lost thousands of miles away and millions of years ago is now awakening to the character of a woman. She will be found. She will discover her destiny — a life that includes being wanted. Clarity will come. The connection she has developed with her creator will deepen. The pain of loss will lessen. In fact, with her newfound awareness, doors will open for her to be kissed with an unparalleled touch of love.

She will discover a stronger sense of her worth.

Listen to the Music

"Daydreaming," by Luke Falkner

Chapter 13

The Kiss

Touch is the heart's way of
telling the truth.

The Kiss

When you kiss me
your magic moves
inside my spirit
searching for an answer

As you kiss me again
I melt
closer into you
until I find a safe place
next to your heart

You kiss me once more
here, you are
my lips meet a soul
a life transforms my existence

Wet waters
warm wishes
soft syllables
sweet

Kisses

Her Story

The Kiss

When kissed with pure love, she feels magic move inside her spirit, and she searches for an answer. "Will you accept the affection that abides in this kiss?" True love seeks a match, a reflection of itself. It embodies the appreciation of another. The kiss represents enjoyment and recognition of her. She is kissed in her language and begins to recognize more of her true self.

As she envelops *the kiss of affection*, she discovers another facet of her value. She feels not only invited into another's world to be enjoyed and recognized for who she is but also accepted, no matter what. She remembers the time she stepped into his office, disgruntled by the disappointment of her day. She was wearing red patent leather high-heeled shoes, a skirt that flared out from the knees, and a pretty white lace blouse tucked in around her tiny waist. She had tears in her eyes.

As she sat down in the chair next to his, he looked at her with adoration. He wore a slight smile. His smile brought comfort. His eyes sparkled with delight. Tears trickled down her face, and he kissed her. In that moment, she knew how much she was appreciated. He admired how she held herself in high regard, for her confidence glowed in the way she dressed; he embraced her sensitive side and her ability to be vulnerable, dispelling tears in disappointment. Most of all, he thought highly of her, for her superpower was humility.

Streams of tears, warm wishes of appreciation, and soft syllables of affirmation emerged from this kiss. Without a touch like this, letting go of past trauma and forming new bonds with the ability to be real would not be possible. She is appreciated for who she is, and healing accelerates.

But there is a sharp turn on the road ahead. Around the corner from the showering light of removal is a dark cloud. Her friend is back, the wolf. This time, he's wearing a heavy black coat of fur — a symbol of pure darkness, a warning of what's to come. In her rearview mirror, she is forced to go back to haunting memories that have lain hidden, deep within her subconscious mind. She must feel the pain of buried emotions and remove hidden cells of trauma, or the demon of destruction could drive her back into oppression.

Her over-striving to obtain a bond with a man to compensate for having none with her parents, is coming to an end.

Listen to the Music

"More Than Words — Extreme," by The Piano Guys and J. Rice

Part 2

Here She Comes

"I know I am in here, but where? I need to get to the other side, but how? I have suffered long enough. I need love. I don't want to be left behind. Take away the curse of entrapment! Break the chains that bind me so! Please, oh please, make my dreams come true."

Listen to the Music

"The Sound of Silence," sung by, Nouela

This piece of music will awaken you to the power of purity that is released when wounds are exposed, pain is felt, and deep-buried emotions are liberated. There is a time for silence and a time to voice the facts: your truth — remembering, that secrets hide the truth, but having the courage to stand up in authenticity releases the oppressed. The hope? Acknowledgment — for this affirms a true reflection of reality as it appears; therefore, the verdict within the mind will rest in peace.

Chapter 14

The Kitchen Sink

Goodbye is not forever,
but a mark that lasts a
lifetime.

The Kitchen Sink

I was washing the dishes, in a hurry to see him
The telephone rang, my dad held the receiver
A blow stung his eyes

The shotgun went off inside my soul
He pulled the trigger, put a rifle to his head
He was still breathing

I ran out the door, towards his house
Instead forced into a truck
Dad drove me around and around

I never got to touch his face
Or listen to his heartbeat, his last breath
Feel my hand on his, fingertip to tip

He called me before we were to meet
Talked and then he said, "Goodbye, I have to go."
He seemed casual, I would see him soon, but I didn't.

I waited for the letter he *must* have sent in the mail
To let me know why he left this place
That he loved me more than this

Two days before he died, I dreamed him riding black horse
I too was with horse, on land of my grandfather,
who passed away years ago

I woke up the next morning, he came to see me
He said, "I sat on carousel, riding a black horse
You beside me, you with a horse."

"Now, I believe, I believe in God."
Before, he was an atheist and never could conceive
Told me love was God and God was lost

Before this, he came to my father pleading to see me
My father told him, "Never return! You're not allowed to be around!"
Young love, made love, a sin to a Catholic, too young. "Jail it would be!"

I remember looking out the kitchen window
Where I would do the dishes, he'd sneak to gaze, to stare, to dream
From the alleyway and round the gate, watching, waiting, hoping, hiding

The day he left, I was going to plead my case
Beg to see him, hope to feel, embrace
But instead, he shot himself — away for good, from me, away from destiny

Years did pass, I never forgot, just like it was yesterday
The difference now? He visits often, always guiding
He descends in dreams, at the edge of my bed and talks to me

When I do the dishes and look out my kitchen window, gaze, stare, dream
I feel he is near — eternally watching, forever waiting, still hoping
No longer hiding. At last, he is here, in spirit he is near.

Her Story

The Kitchen Sink

She was 15 years old and in high school. Shaken by the trials of everyday family life and bullied by female schoolmates who hated her appearance, caused her to isolated from adolescent experiences. She was constantly in a chronic state of stress. She was not able to relax or be open to enjoying her youth. Anxiety and fear surrounded her, in the same way, swarming wasps subdue their prey and inject poison into flesh. She was always on guard. To be honest, she wasn't allowed to have normal exchanges with friends, partially because she was highly controlled by her father. And this embarrassed her. She was too nervous to bring friends home. She worried about how she would be treated in front of them. Would he throw her up against the wall for laughing too loud, like he had at her thirteenth birthday party? Or listen in on conversations with the hope of catching some dirt on her and proving she was the bad one?

She was far from *being bad.* Her nature was quite gentle and sweet. She was stunning to look at and a threat to those with low self-esteem. She had long, blonde, curly hair, athletic curves, and ocean-blue eyes that shone sincerity, and sophistication beyond the average look. In school, even though she didn't give the boys much attention, girls still called her a slut. They would follow her down the hallways, pretending to cough while breathing out slanderous words. Everyone heard. It was so humiliating. She began to believe it was true.

The bullying didn't stop there. Walking home from school meant a punch in the head or the threat of being beaten up. It was hard to get out of bed in the morning — thoughts of facing the tyranny of mean girls made her sick, and going home at the end of the day was tense and depressing. She was defamed and blamed for being something she wasn't: a slut and a bad girl. How did she deserve this guilty sentence? She felt helpless in the face of her perpetrators. Fierceness was not in her nature. She was taught to be "the good girl" and didn't know how to stand up for herself. She feared punishment more than the challenge of confronting her enemies. Chronic stress is trauma, and it paralyzes the one experiencing it.

In the middle of this exhausted state of being, she met her first love. He turned out to be her lifesaver.

His care was unconditional and his affection was sweet bliss. They were both in high school when they met. He was two years her senior. Tall, blonde, and handsome. He too had ocean-blue eyes, which pierced her like a spell and made her feel special. He owned a green Chevy muscle truck that she loved so much, just about as much as him! She found great enjoyment and freedom sitting next to him when driving around town — speeding fast on newly paved roads and taking slow midnight excursions down gravel country roads.

Spending time with him took her far away from her troubles. Ongoing abuse stole pleasure from a heart that wanted to play, but by the grace of love, he brought her immense joy. Time stood still with him. She never wanted to leave his side. But the hands of time ticked quickly away. Within the short-lived existence he had to offer her, she learned much about maturity.

He taught her how to cook. He had deadly skills when it came to preparing food. He walked her through barbecuing the best pork chops ever and how to make the creamiest cheese sauce for hot, steamy rice. He was forever showing her new things. When he taught her how to drive, he was patient and gentle with instructions. He didn't even get mad when she hit the back of a car with his front bumper.

He always had time for her. He loved her. Young love *is* true love.

After some time, they became intimate. His mother found out by walking in on them in the bedroom, although they didn't know at the time. It was in the middle of the afternoon, and supposedly she had come home from work on her lunch break. Perturbed about the whole ordeal and unsettled with the fact her son was dating someone from the opposite side of the tracks, his mother told her parents. Her father reamed her out and said she could never see him again. The rigidity of the news crushed them both. But her boyfriend pursued seeing her anyway. He was her protector, and he wasn't leaving her.

He made sure she got home from school safely. He stood up for her when others defamed her. He protected her from bullies at parties and the mall. She was safe with him. He created freedom. And when she was called a slut, he made it clear who he believed in. However, her father found out he was still seeing her, and he threatened to send him to jail. He was 17, and she was 15, a minor in the eyes of the law.

She remembers the past with him, like it was yesterday, how he came to talk it out with her father. They weren't bad kids. They were young adults in love, pursuing goals and with a clear direction in mind. She watched out her living room window as he stood — tall, confident, and courageous — facing a man filled with rage. He was wearing his best pink sweater, tan dress pants, and fancy brown leather shoes. He looked like an advocate coming to plead a case worth arguing. His strong character, yet soft eyes, sent a message of sensibility, with the hope to win.

But he lost the trial. Young love was crushed.

"I will send you to jail if you ever see her again!" her father raged. The following day, she was to visit his parents and bring forward her plea, but he shot himself in the head with a shotgun just before she was due to arrive. She was in the middle of doing the dishes at the kitchen sink, a job she had to finish before going to his house. When she was almost done, the phone rang. It was her boyfriend's stepfather. He told her dad she could not come over and why.

He had pressed the barrel of a rifle under the hood of his neck and pulled the trigger. The bullet tore through layers of bone and skin, lodging itself into the fibres of his brain. She was told that he was still breathing when the police arrived.

She was not allowed to see him, touch him, or hold his hand. No final farewell.

After his death, she went numb and shut down. A time in her youth that was meant for discovery and the blossoming of promises to come to life, turned into hell on earth. The shock of it all froze her in time. He had been her only means of joy, freedom, and escape. And in one quick breath, he was gone. He had stood strong in the battle for her, but he couldn't handle the loss and took his life instead.

Every single day, in that very same year of his passing, she looked in the mailbox for a letter, a note from him explaining *why* he had chosen to leave. But the square red mailbox, what appeared to be her only passageway to hope, remained empty. When the denial of his departure vanished and reality sunk in, her spirit hid for a very long time.

A few years later, she moved into her own home. The very first time she did the dishes in her kitchen sink and looked out the window towards the alleyway, he appeared. His face reminded her of their young love. As she looked out the window again, he spoke to her: "I am with you, so close and forever near." Although crushed in spirit and her heart a bleeding mess, in that moment, she felt young again.

She thought... Was he the wolf? The voice of wisdom in her dreams? The symbol of protection? She wondered because the wolf always appeared to her when a predator was nearby.

She put down the dish that she was washing to go play their favourite song.

Listen to the Music

"Everything I Do, I Do It For You," by Brian Adams

Chapter 15

Crushed

Nurture the broken
hearted with endearment,
for it brings sunshine to
the soul.

Crushed

I am not open
To
Feel
Anymore

I lie on warm sand
A hot summer day
The heat burns my body
Yet, I do not feel its fire

I don't want to feel
I'd rather the sun scorch away my pain
Eat the flesh from my body
Reminders of days, months, years

Times, hours, minutes, seconds
Smells, seasons, recollections
I don't want to feel the pricks
Of darkness, heartache

I wish for a warm summer's day
Heat the sand around me
Burn misery into embers, ashes
Eat memories away

Reminders of school bullies, men
Siblings, parents, officers, teachers
All who stole my spirit, worth
Intrinsic value, my spark — left to doubt

I am gone now
Dead to me
Numb to the world
Society believes they have no part

No influence, no illness
But NO! *They* are weak!
Insane. Sick. Not *me*.
I am only fifteen. Vulnerable

I am not open
To
Feel
Anymore

Her Story

Crushed

The spirit of a girl has been crushed. Early beginnings wreaked havoc on later years. Her soul carries intense trauma, and she doesn't want to feel the emotional pain anymore. Bad memories sit dormant in her body, and they need to come out. This has caused her to separate from her childlike, joyful self. But she finds comfort in nature. She lies in the sun, hoping the heat will burn away memories causing her despondency. She is detached from her true self because her spirit is crushed.

As she lies on the warm sand, the sun beating her body with its heat and hot rays of sunshine brightening her face, she hopes for a miracle to free her. But memories just don't melt away that easily. Her spark was blown out. Of course, she's going to feel dead to the world! If only others would just acknowledge their wrongdoing! Wouldn't that make things better?

She reflects on her childhood. When she was six years old, she knew the truth. She just wasn't given permission to express it. She saw things for how they were. Yet, it was impossible to communicate verbally the wisdom in her mind, because her reality would be denied. So, she shut down. She understood that the sin of others was not her fault. But the insanity of their lack of acknowledgment caused her to doubt her own mind and intuition. A seed of doubt caused her to sink into a great depression, but she didn't realize this at the time. A child needs to be heard, understood, and affirmed. If a child is ignored, she will doubt her reality, detach from her feelings and emotions, and become despondent.

Once a little girl, now a woman, entering the pain of a numb and paralyzed state, she realizes she has a chance to scream out for help. By doing so, she can let go and expose the past, connect to her fragmented child within, and build a new home for her identity – a place where plenty of sunshine can enter. Undeniably, she will face harsh realities along the way. But she's worth the journey of exposure and release.

She feels so alone, but she will make it, anyway.

Listen to the Music

"I Wanna Dance With Somebody Who Loves Me," sung by
Morgan Harper-Jones

Chapter 16

No Home

A foundation exists
where it is first built;
therefore, build wisely, and
the frame of your life will
forever stand strong.

No Home

I try, but there's nowhere to go
I'm trapped and feel so alone
I look for a door, one that opens
And fits my broken frame

I pursue, building amongst the rubble
The same old mess, cleaned up a dozen times before
But the nails hinder me
Bent way beyond repair

Why not lay bricks and build my very own house?
A home like glue, secure
Is familiarity better than freedom?
Stuck, for the unknown scares me so

Yet, hard to live in a wasteful mess
To make clear, a concise way out
More so, to go out a door
never framed in the first place

Her Story

No Home

Time and time again, she tries to leave her hometown, where tragedy sits on every street corner as an unfriendly reminder of the past. Each attempt causes her to freeze. She's scared that she won't be enough to make it on her own. She feels trapped in an environment that's never been home in the first place. So why this resistance? The trauma of an insecure attachment in childhood brings on a state of fear when moving towards freedom. In the past, freedom was met with punishment. She had to sneak out of the house to have a life and do the things normal teenagers did. But she would get caught. And when she did, she was met with rage and forced to clean the house into all hours of the night. Her body became a prison, and she couldn't escape. So instead of looking for a new home, she looks for a door with a keyhole that matches her distorted frame of mind.

Amongst the rubble of her past, she struggles to build a life in the same old house of pain — a mess she's tried to clean up a thousand times before. Trying to create happiness in a home where the foundation is built on bent nails, a place of absolute dysfunction, only hinders her from achieving freedom. Old, ingrained, and unhealthy mindsets create repeating patterns of behavior without yielding positive, healthy results.

Amid her fatigue, she begins to seriously question herself. "Why not lay bricks and build my very own house?" she wonders. "Why not reach freedom by creating my destiny?" She begins to imagine building her own home, one with a foundation that represents security — the glue that holds the heart of a home together.

Yet, she still doubts. Should she settle for the familiar? In a weird and distorted way, it feels comfortable. Freedom is so unfamiliar, and it feels eons away — untouchable. Freedom is unknown to her, and the unknown scares her. It reminds her of that yucky feeling just before something bad happens. She needs to let go of these feelings and the emotion attached to being stuck: fear.

As she tunes into this reality, aware that she's wasting precious time building a house of dreams in the rubble of a mess, she leaves. But just as she gets ready to go, she is struck with a conflicting thought. "I can't leave a home, go out a door that was never framed with love in the first place." How does she leave a place she called home that was never home, to begin with?

She must reimagine her home and reinvent her mansion. She must build a foundation of truth that is strong, rather than a crumbling one that is weak. She must work hard to get rid of the double-edged sword that has created a heart of duplicity.

Listen to the Music

"Home," by Philip, Philips, and The Piano Guys

Chapter 17

Bipolar in Me

Duplicity stems from two sides: yours and another. Choose you.

Bipolar in Me

There once was a girl
touched with
DUPLICITY
those near, closest to her
half-handed offered
loving, tender care
It peeped out,
a glimmer of hope
seen from the corner of her eye
only to breathe

In the next breath...

A hot and humid
sweaty palm,
full of harm
mean, spiteful
harsh, contemptuous
a heart filled with hate
leaving her
confused, unstable, insecure
DECEPTION
is not
love

Years later...

She would lose her shit while driving
pound the steering wheel
scream at the injustice
holler out,
"Why this JUDAS KISS? How it betrays me so!"
Hit another pothole

Woke up! Again
in the house of an abuser
burning her hair
long locks of blonde curls

Took the life from her...

It was SHE who could not leave
conditions of entrapment
built upon a collected
recycling of dysfunctional people
a pattern from childhood
She was good at wailing
in the cycle of
HYPOCRISY
a well-practiced
repeat victim

Powerless...

Healthy one day
take care of self
Exercise, eat vegetables, meditate
Abused the next
neglect self
Eat six burgers, gain weight, starve
allow the yelling, ignore the glare
rebuke the insults, silence the lamb
After all this
sulk in bed

"Her and I together
must escape this DUPLICITY!"

Her Story

Bipolar in Me

She revisits the effects of duplicity, the brainwashing from double-minded people, who coerced her into believing that their dysfunction was acceptable and her responsibility to carry. Their acts of half-handedness fell short of giving her what she needed, and the perpetuation of abuse caused her to separate from her true self. Those near and closest to her had a responsibility to love, protect, and earn her trust. But they didn't. Because of this, she diverged from her *true self.*

In her younger years, she hoped and prayed that the bite-sized morsels of affection would remain. But those with personality and character disorders forced her to endure contempt, hate, and harm. Time and time again, an abusive hand struck her heart and mind. On occasion, droplets of tenderness were offered. Like her grandfather's love — she could feel it in his smile and warm touch. He gave the best hugs. Most other times, though, rainstorms of harshness poured down. Her grandfather rejected her for being a young mother. He refused to hold her daughter as a baby.

The ironic dichotomy of two different worlds created different sides to her personality: a peaceful side, amid hope for stability, and a confused side, amid abuse. The contempt she absorbed was much greater than the love she received. How could she feel her grandfather's deep and energetic love, knowing he was fond of her yet later in life refused to hold her child? Such confusion overwhelmed her. She didn't know what to think or do with this duplicity. Confusion caused a *splitting* of her personality and forced instructive emotions to hide.

On the contrary, as she enters womanhood, the pull of duplicity causes emotions to explode! The residue of uncertainty brings heat to an already overloaded nervous system. An underlying current of anger and bitterness is ignited when she feels cornered. Never before able to express natural feelings in response to acts of unkindness, she now explodes when triggered.

Her car becomes a safe place to vent, and she frequently loses it while driving. Her reaction to hitting potholes triggers memories of injustice from the past. "Why this JUDAS KISS? How it betrays me so!" The Judas kiss… the ultimate act of betrayal amid a deceptive and skillful disguise of love. Every pothole reminds her of the discomfort she feels while carrying baggage from the past, all of which has influenced her cycle of dysfunctional choices.

She continues to put herself into the hands and under the houses of abusers. Stuck in high gear, trying to escape the familiarity of dysfunction but with little success, she drives herself to the point of madness and exhaustion. She has a hard time escaping conditions of entrapment, a bosom-friendly familiarity. In an attempt to warm her heart with love, she does the bipolar opposite. She builds a recycled collection of maladjusted relationships, a pattern learned in childhood as permissible. She continues spinning hamster wheels by acting out learned behaviors from the past.

Through her lack of knowledge and awareness, she suffers the pain of hypocrisy and becomes a repeat victim of her circumstances. As an adult, the destructive choices she makes cause further victimization, leaving her feeling powerless and unstable.

She attempts to take care of herself: exercising often, eating good food, participating in daily meditation, and rejecting insults. All of these become a part of her healthy regime. Nevertheless, she needs more for inner transformation to occur. Without proper guidance and genuine emotional support, she slips right back into performing self-destructive habits. She allows abuse, endures passive aggression, and ignores the red flags of narcissism. Her perpetrators use emotional tyranny to gain the upper hand and control her life. Like a helpless lamb, she is silenced.

At this point, the only safe place to release pain is in her bed, when she cries herself to sleep. Under such duress, she internalizes the magnitude of duplicity, the double-mindedness that has made her mad. She wants to eliminate the baggage collected from others so she can connect to who she is. What she cannot deny is that she has developed two personalities: hers and another.

To find her way, she has to admit her reality: there are two sides to her story.

Listen to the Music

"You Learn," by Alanis Morissette

Chapter 18

Binocular Vision

To lose your power is to hand it over to a fool.

Binocular Vision

I am an abused woman
denial no more, hitherto
eyes wide open, binocular vision
owl stare, deep black holes
lead me to the unknown

SUFFERING!

Here I am, but I'm going
feels strange to leave
got to go for the good
out of the death stare
into the night, lamp light!

BRIGHT!

Every step feels heavy
a depressive drug seeping
into feet – need to move
brain fighting against old
chains of oppressive control

SIGHT!

Lantern bright! Guide me out
vision on High, above
restore my power, once more
strength to become one of those
HOO, HOO sees!

Her Story

Binocular Vision

It is one thing to be a fool in love. It's another to hand your power over to a fool. A fool is someone unpredictable and unwilling to learn. They are the most dangerous people to be around. They can turn on you without a moment's notice. They can be highly abusive. In an abusive relationship, external power is handed over to the fool, and inner power fades away. As adults, we have a choice: to leave an abusive relationship or not. Denial keeps one stuck, blinding one to the severity and effects of abuse. Yet, it is equally important to understand that it takes great strength to leave.

When a woman admits to being abused, she releases the power an abuser has over her and, at the same time, recognizes her vulnerability. She no longer denies her reality. She is fed up with allowing herself to be victimized. She puts on her *wise owl-like vision*, which allows her to see far into the distance of this dark reality, a reality called suffering, and beyond the horizon. She owns these deep, black holes of despair, reflected in an owl's stare, yet they also provide binocular vision, an awakening to a new reality.

For her, it feels strange to leave a life that had been so familiar. But she also knows if she doesn't leave, she will die. She decides to go after the *good*. At the same time, leaving feels like death. An abrupt change from abuse to freedom can bring on grief and an overwhelming fear of the unknown. Crossing over is like heading into the precarity of night.

The journey towards light is tough. Every step of the way, while letting go of the past, feels heavy, like a depressive drug numbing the soles of her feet. It's hard to move from what is underneath — conditions of *old.* But she makes a choice. The choice is hers. She chooses to reprogram her mind. Play different tapes. Hence, she calls out for help.

"Lantern bright, guide me out! Restore my power once more!" She asks to be filled with clear vision, like that of an owl who can see far into the distance — a guide to bring her to the other side. Freedom lives there.

She will learn how to fly above the mess and see through the suffering, elevating her consciousness.

Listen to the Music

"Blackbird," by The Beatles

Chapter 19

So Messed Up, But Not

To not know thyself is a curse; a burden be unto me.

So Messed Up, But Not

I want what I want
but I don't *really* know
what I want
my heart and my head
are so fucked up
separated in two
too hard to know
what I need, is all
and what needs me
and how much to give
or give nothing at all
maybe a little?
hoping confusion
leaves this brain,
and my heart wakes up
wakes me up good
like the morning sun
when she kisses the sky
and brightens the day
brings more than hope
through hot sunny rays
I want what I want
but I don't *really* know
what I want
my heart and my head
are so fucked up
but not too much.

(She smiles)

Her Story

So Messed Up, But Not

Unless one is raised in a cycle of insanity, it's not normal for their head and their heart to become disconnected from one another. But if that happens, the result is confusion. When confusion becomes the common denominator in every choice and decision needing clarity, another disconnect occurs. You question your values, the opinion of others, and your morals, and you doubt your boundaries and whether they are even apparent in the first place. Self-doubt is a miserable place to be.

The constant self-questioning drives her crazy, to the point where she interrogates her sanity. Despite this, she recognizes and hopes that just maybe, she's not all that messed up. Talking out the madness helps her. Releasing emotions, feelings, and thoughts — the good, the bad, and the ugly is like shining a bright light toward the end of a dark tunnel. Even though she doesn't know what she wants or what to do right now, she will eventually figure it out.

Deep down inside the gut of her intuition, she trusts that life is good. In the same way the morning sun brightens the sky with a kiss of newness, she trusts the sun's warmth will nurture growth and sustainability into her life. She finds a sense of relief after letting go of her feelings. At the end of the day, she smiles her confusion, doubt, and insanity away with the realization that she is normal. She just needs to let go and be.

Listen to the Music

"Older," by Sasha Sloan

Chapter 20

Forbidden Assault

The face of evil is the
love you desperately desire,
hidden under a mask of
destruction, destroying
pure intent!

Forbidden Assault

I thought it was love, real
I wanted it to be
I was so deprived
I liked how
It felt

His seductive forbidden body language, scary
His large form near mine
His hand inside shirt
His eyes staring
On me

Those charming looks turned into fantasy
Those lips kissed me passionately
Those arms held me
Those thighs wrapped
Me tight

Attention caressed empty mortality, bliss
Attention fondled every trouble away
Attention relieved lonely boredom
Attention warmed
My insides

Until my eyes opened wide, sizably
Until something seemed very off
Until his haunting past
Until the others
Came forward

I thought it was love, real
I wanted it to be
I was so deprived
I hate now
The truth

Her Story

Forbidden Assault

She wanted to believe it was true, that he loved her. She trusted his intentions were pure, for hers were. Never did she imagine, even in the scariest parts of her imagination, how bad things were! The distraction from truth came from her enjoyment of how he handled her. His tattooed hands touched her with such skill and precision, an art perfected for priming her into the palm of his hand. It was as though he knew her desires better than she knew herself. She enjoyed the feeling of turning flush, her temperature rising, and the palpable pulse of blood flowing through her veins. Of course she did. This is what love looked like in her youth.

He lured her with sexual affection, an enticing distraction from the truth. He *groomed* her to believe that pleasure, perpetuating dependency, was love, not lust. His goal was to get her attached so she'd believe his lies and become dependent on him. When he first spotted her, she wore a look of deprivation — the kind that develops from lack of attention and neglect. Layered wounds from her past were transparent on her face, making her vulnerable to prey. Purple broken veins, deep red bruises, and blackened blood-stained tears shone for predators like a bright star.

This made it easy for him to calculate her weaknesses, knowing exactly how to work his game until she was caught — hook, line, and sinker. He used his body to seduce her with a forbidden fruit that felt scary at first, yet strangely exciting and familiar. He offered her a thrill of heightened ecstasy, mixed with emotional bonding and gifts of strong-smelling perfume, a forewarning of the stench to come. Fooled into believing *assault* was romance and love, she fell hard and fast, landing on betrayal. She became blinded by a diabolical nature that turned lies into truth.

Like no other, he caressed her breasts with tenderness, arousing past trauma away. He wrapped his thick legs around her, like a layer of comfort, promising he'd never leave. His jet-black eyes mingled with the dark hole in her soul, making amicable their connection and heightening their provocatively seductive interactions. His intimate charm turned false love into a world of fantasy and believability. His undivided, round-the-clock attention caressed her lonely soul. Her mortality became filled with bliss. The attention he gave removed boredom from her mundane life. He warmed her insides with attention, staying as close to her as often as he could.

And then it happened. Without warning. The bomb dropped on her lap and broke her heart. A phone call came in. The voice on the other end of the receiver confirmed who he *really* was. Without a doubt, her eyes were opened to his haunting past: the children he sexually molested. The women he assaulted and raped. The violent attacks toward those he said he loved.

After the first phone call, she began an in-depth investigation to find out more. Victims came forward. This confirmed her relationship was a lie, a falsehood of her perception. She'd thought it was real love, a romance made in heaven. She'd wanted it to be. She was so deprived. Unfortunately, to her emotional detriment, she had to admit the betrayal of her experience.

She hated the truth. How painful it was to reflect on every moment of their time together, a loophole of lies! But it all started making sense. And *why* she was here, at this moment. She had to see and feel the pain she had forgotten in her childhood, as an adult, to understand. His sick ways brought back the memory of a twelve-year-old girl's tragedy. She finally felt the sliver buried deep within and saw its mark: the surgeon who had molested her.

She wasn't quite ready to face the facts.

Listen to the Music

"The Heart Asks Pleasure First," by Michael Nyman

Chapter 21

Get Out

Listen! Your inner voice
of repetition never lies.

Get Out

The closer we got
The farther away we became
Long distance scorned our souls
Time and space
Became us, detached
It hurt

But why?

When you arrived
Close
And closer
Closer still
We lost touch
Talked less

Loved little
Laughed
Not so much
Wanting you nearer
Tore us apart

You leaving
When we'd just met
Broke my heart
Ripped it in two
Until I did not know
What to do…

But leave.

You told me
To let you in
Let go, love
Let me love you
I, on the other hand
Felt distraught

But why?

There was something
In between
My spirit sensed
Mind, unsure
Heart, resistant
Soul, nervous

It wasn't good
Hidden, secrets
An actor at heart
A diabolical breed, born,
Maybe made in-house?
Hard to say for sure

But leave.

Her Story

Get Out

As normal becomes more familiar to her, repetitive and intuitive thoughts grip firmer at her heartstrings, making clear the truth. Once separated by long distance, the closer in proximity she becomes with her new boyfriend, the more she realizes that time and space are not what divide her from him. It is his diabolical nature. Spending more time with him causes her to distance herself emotionally. Physical distance is no longer a form of contention in their relationship. There are other disturbing reasons.

The signs are apparent now. Easily seen. Clear as day. They talk less, love little, and laugh with much restraint. The growing separation between them is confusing to her but completely real. Multiple attempts to reconnect to the *spark* that once lit the couple like two dry wicks seem to tear them further apart. They were a magnetic force in the first months of getting to know each other. Now, her pursuit of a deeper emotional connection causes his anger to rise. He's afraid of being found out.

She initially felt torn by the physical separation that took place when he abruptly left town for work. The exit shocked her. She wanted him near as they were blossoming into a love-filled couple. She knew in her heart that distance would not grow a relationship. But little did she know that distance was the very thing saving her from drowning into a pool of despair. There it was again, that unpredictable anger, igniting without warning.

She knew something wasn't right, despite their gravitation towards each other. Her mind grew sure, her heart less resistant to intuition, and she came to see her anxiety as a gift. Time and space revealed an actor at large. He danced to a wicked tune — a liar at heart, identically matched to his nature at birth, a genetic disposition prone to sociopathy, and a childhood wound of neglect that had burnt a scar of narcissism into his heart. She knew she had to leave. She would not try to change him. Even though a strange and magnetic spark burned so bright, she had to follow her gut instincts and get out.

Something familiar about him reminded her of her past, a dark side of her life that lay dormant in her memory. She remembered the wolf who came to warn her in a dream. His black coat of fur shook aloud in her mind, symbolic of her dark past, the one she had to shake off.

They had crossed paths for a reason. It was time for her to remember the deep-rooted trauma that had first stolen her childlike innocence. She could no longer run from her pain. The scar across her abdomen was a reminder of what separated her from the truth. She had suffered far too long and was about to remember *why.*

All in a memory, cycles of prolonged suffering will soon come to an end.

Listen to the Music

"Liber Tango," Performed by Bandoneon

Part 3

Coming Alive

"I loved him. I thought I loved him. And then, I learned to hate him. He was a monster in disguise. A two-faced snake. A molester. One who had raped women, just like I was raped when I was a young girl. I never thought I would feel another breath down my neck that resembled the past. Now, I have no choice but to remember if I want to heal. Almost half a lifetime searching for me; little did I know I had to let go of them."

Chapter 22

Molester, Me Away

Prestige and position are
no excuse to get away with
wicked abuse.

Molester, Me Away

The molester hid his sin in me
Made me full of shame
A doctor was his name

Woke up after surgery
More oxygen on my face?
Kind of my saving grace

For I can only remember bits
Pieces of the story, memory went away
Where my drugged body lay

His fingers deep inside
Going in and out, so hard they pricked
Prestige hid his sickly gain

Took the organ out, he shouldn't
An excuse to feel inside
Sustain his jolly hard rise

Hid his depression in me
A burden carried for so long
He stole my song — away I went

Her Story

Molester, Me Away

She woke up earlier than usual this morning to a deep, throbbing stomach pain. Her mother took her to the doctor. The doctor referred her to a surgeon. The insanity of the situation was that both her mother and her doctor couldn't figure out the *real reason* for her pain. It was the tribulation of her first menstrual cycle. She didn't realize that her groans of agony and gripping abdominal cramps were the results of a natural change in life.

As quickly as she was booked into a hospital room, under the instruction of Dr. Chan, she felt the absence of her mother. She was left alone. Where had her mother gone? And *why* did she leave her alone? Her body was rolled down a dark, dreary corridor on a hard, metal stretcher. A nurse pushed her into the surgical room, where she was told to remove her clothing. In a short moment, a sharp blade with a long silver handle hung from the hand of an aggressive nurse who tore at her skin, one section at a time, removing her pubic hair. The removal of her hair frightened her. She didn't know what was going to happen next.

With each scrape of the blade, a tear ran down her face. She felt violated, lying stark naked, fully exposed to an insensitive nurse who ignored her vulnerability. Fear loomed in the atmosphere like a demon lurking in the night, waiting to devour his prey. When the lights in the room went dim, she was out. The anesthesia rendered her unconscious, and during the surgery, they removed a fallopian tube.

Upon waking, she felt extreme pinching pains inside her vagina, only to find the surgeon pounding his palm against her exposed skin, hard fingers in between her legs, forcefully moving them in and out. He beat her insides to shreds with his sharp fingers. Just as she was about to scream out for help, his yellow hand came towards her face, holding a clear plastic mask filled with medicine to drug her.

Silent. Silent. Silent.

The way men liked her.

He removed her fallopian tube in compensation for a moment to feel good. He robbed her of her innocence. She left the hospital depressed. Removed from self. Where was her mother? Why didn't she stay with her?

She, too, wore the mask of silence.

The spirit of a girl entered the hospital as one person and left as another. Looking back, she now understands *why* she left her body, became detached from herself, and searched for her soul under an unbuckled belt of the con man — the place where a dark secret lay tucked away.

Listen to the Music

"Vocalise," Op. 34, No. 14, by Sergei Rachmaninoff,
sung by Anna Moffo

Chapter 23

Lights Out!

A better man does not
return changed unless he
wants to get better and
commits to his betterment.
Measure carefully your
desire for him to return.

Lights Out!

Violation no more!
You WILL NOT touch me
When you think you have the right
Beyond MY ability to choose
Numb my responses, DULL my instincts
BETRAY trust, turn innocence to lust
Hold me down as **soul departs**
NO thrill, a CRIME!
You will NOT take what's MINE!

Pervert
Narcissist
Addict
Aggressor
Controller
Monster
Rapist
Sex-addict
Violator
Psychopath
Sociopath
Liar
Hypocrite
Charmer
Actor
Rake
Enchanter
Snake
Fake
Convincer
Perpetrator

Violation no more!
You WILL NOT touch me
When you think you have the right
Beyond MY ability to choose
Numb my responses, DULL my instincts
BETRAY trust, turn innocence to lust
Hold me down as **soul departs**
NO THRILL, a CRIME!
You will NOT take what's MINE!

LIGHTS OUT!

Her Story

Lights Out!

What more is there to say? Lights out to abuse; meaning, enough is enough. She turns her light back on so the dark side cannot touch her with the debris and disillusionment of distraction and destruction. At this moment, she reflects on the most prominent reason for a life of pain: repeat patterns of unhealthy learned behaviour and long-term exposure to dark shadows that blind heart sight and silenced expression.

She is connecting to emotional maturity, wisdom, and good sense.

Listen to the Music

"When You Wish Upon a Star," by Cliff Edwards

Chapter 24

Three Times Gone

To be aware is confusion
gone — the new normal
is back in style.

Three Times Gone

I was loved three times.
Not for very long.

The first, I didn't know.
The second, I let him go.
The third was a tragedy.

I never knew love, the first. My eyes
could not see.

I lost sight of the second. I turned
away from thee.

I never loved a man more, than the third. His
warm heart was nearest me

In an instant, he was gone.
The star's sparkle as she shone, vanished.

Lack of awareness strikes me
Like lightning, its thunder warns me
Another relationship, three times gone.

Her Story

Three Times Gone

She's almost there. Isn't she? Just a few more memories to process. Her heart needs more time to make sense out of unsettling memories. During her upbringing, she was taught to believe that if you had sex before marriage, you were a sinner. Guilty. A disgrace. On the other hand, marriage was the answer to sanctifying sex. She was indoctrinated with the ideology that marriage as an institution and under particular religious beliefs secured sex as pure and upright. But without such walls, it is a violation of the female body, a fornication of the will of God and a dismemberment of the body of believers.

Considering she had sex out of marriage, the last thing she wanted to feel was guilt. She ignored the small, still voice from within to avoid scorn. She married men who were not suitable for her to avoid condemnation. It takes time to get to know yourself and learn to follow your heart for the heart tells the truth. But sometimes, the truth is hard to digest. And when you're young and come from a dysfunctional background, a *bad* man may look pretty *good*. On the other hand, she hadn't even had a chance to find herself.

As she walks down the church aisle of her first marriage, she hears a whisper alerting her. A voice deep within tells her to stop. *Something isn't right.* Her heart, intuition, and maybe an angel on her side is speaking to her. But she doesn't quite understand why she shouldn't proceed. She is young and a bit naïve. She does not question what she cannot see. But logic doesn't always tell the truth. More so, her need for love and attachment is too intense to see through the mirage of deception.

Shortly after getting married, she discovers her husband had been with another woman at the time of their courtship. He cheated on her before marriage, and his best friend told her two months after the wedding. She never told him she knew. She, herself, was in denial. She was waiting for a hard-copy moment. She had to plan a safe exit for herself and her son, even though her ex-husband stabbed her in the back later on in life by fooling her son into leaving his mother — to escape his financial responsibilities as he was going through another divorce.

The second attempt at finding a lasting relationship is a big mistake. After marriage, her partner reveals characteristics that are psychopathic. He hid them well when they were dating. He was a real churchgoer, dedicated to reading the Bible and attending biblical group studies. But behind closed doors, when no one else was looking, if he wasn't in control, his rage turned red like fire. He hid it well, but behind closed doors when no one else was looking, he turned into another man. In the back of his truck, on a trip into the United States, he attempted to kill her by almost breaking her neck. He left her, almost lifeless, with a black and blue body. Before marriage, there were no danger signs, or red flags, except one: he was always nice.

She thought she could turn away from making a mistake a third time. After two bad relationships, wouldn't she see the signs of a con man? Wasn't the pain from her past enough to see through a Jekyll and Hyde character?

In choosing her third relationship, she honestly believes she is in a good place to make a healthy decision. He is carefree, motivating, and cheery. He likes to have fun, and that excites her. Fun wasn't something she experienced for a long time. She believes she could never love a man more. But she soon realizes that a temporary thrill of excitement and a husband who lacks commitment don't work well together. She soon realizes that her husband is not capable of bonding deeply. She tells him she needs more than an on-the-surface connection, and in an instant, he is gone. Her pursuit of deep intimacy in this marriage wasn't something he was capable of giving.

In the end, multiple attempts to secure love leave her without a man by her side. The sparkle in her eye vanishes as quickly as the night sky fades away into the early morning. Her pain and feelings of defeat strike her like a lightning bolt, reminding her to see what changes she needs to make in her own life. The men she chose were con men, the quiet, silent, type and very good at lying. But she is the common denominator, and she must get out of this pattern. Her pain pushes her to seek discernment.

Change is hard. It's the most uncomfortable place to be.

Listen to the Music

"Gone With the Wind," by Julie London

Chapter 25

The Comfort Lump

Dreaming change will emerge when reality speaks otherwise is like tucking yourself into a murky slumber and never waking up.

The Comfort Lump

My bed will never
feel
again, the same

Its place, of comfort
replaced
with, a dent

Your ghost body lay
near
my broken heart

The absence of you
shapes
lump, in throat

If I keep the dent
deep
your ghost, lump

Perhaps there is a chance
you
will, return soon

I need to get a
new
bed, to stay sane

Her Story

The Comfort Lump

She reflects on the men she has chosen and the time she invested in trying to change how they treated her. It hadn't been worth it. The dent left in her bed, emptiness, by men who slept by her side, is a constant reminder of the ghostly presence of hurt, loneliness, and abandonment.

Utilizing every moment of her life to stabilize love, gain security, remove an insecure attachment, and fill a sad heart with a false sense of happiness gnaws at her. Much of her energy is used to clear out multiple ghost-like presences: loss, anxiety, and regret. It is hard for her to sleep at night. Her soul is restless. The absence of love and the dreadful feeling of unfulfillment increase in intensity. Her motivation lessens, making it difficult to leave the bed she has made, the consequences of her actions, and so she falls right back into the deep dent of *familiarity.* She hoped for a different outcome. But hoping isn't enough. She's afraid to feel the pain. Pain means endless suffering. It is not a means to an end.

Yet instead, as she reflects on the pain of insanity. She feels its magnitude and the entirety of its weight, the oppression it causes and the severe consequences attached to it. She decides to end the cycle of pain. Instead, she decides to get a new bed, one without a dent, and perform different ways of being. She will continue to grieve the pain like feathers being plucked from raw flesh, to get to a place where she can say *goodnight* to old ways.

She will no longer enter a slumber with her eyes wide shut.

Listen to the Music

"Easy On Me," by Adele

Chapter 26

Sad Choices Can Change

Pain can awaken you
toward true consciousness.
Become aware, and you
will be illuminated. See,
feel, accept, embrace —
let go.

Sad Choices Can Change

I am so sad
So many things did not work out
Marriage
My hair
Losing children
Peaceful air

I am so sad
So many things did not work out
Relationships
My music
Sibling friendship
Vocal acoustics

I am so sad
So many things did not work out
Jobs
My self-esteem
Stable connections
High school teams

I am so sad
So many things did not work out
Religion
My snobbery
Fixed ideologies
Mindful robberies

I am so sad
So many things did not work out
Fun
My playful years
The candy store
Grasping what is best

Sad choices
Wherever they originated from…
Generational baggage
My footing
Old patterns
Flings of things

It is time to make a change.

Her Story

Sad Choices Can Change

As she says a final farewell to the many things that didn't work out, she creates a list and burns it, extinguishing the past into ashes — burying her pain in the dust. The trauma and its torment, this injustice, will no longer touch her. She can feel the pain leave. She doesn't forget. It just doesn't have the same hold on her anymore. Moving forward, she is free to fly high above the chaos and away from the dark night of her soul. She has learned to cry out for help if she needs it, to say *no* to the bad guy, to make choices that feel right in her heart, and to let go.

Her reflection of the past is just a memory, no longer her present reality. Now that she has made a deliberate decision to move beyond a painful past, she must create change, one step at a time, to transform her future. New habits need to be formed, old and familiar ways removed, healthy friendships embraced, and activities she loves attended to.

Change is all about performing new ways of being and trusting what you see when you look in the mirror. If what she sees represents her true identity, then she can move forward. If what she sees doesn't represent who she is, she can stop and make another choice. Even though she experienced abandonment in her past, she can choose to not abandon herself in the future.

Listen to the Music

"Reflection," by Christina Aguilera

Part 4

Here She Is

"I never knew how much I carried until I began to let the baggage go. I stuffed the craziness into deep, dark closets and buried the chaos into a swollen womb of entrapment. I need the key to unlock the door to my identity, the one that was already open, yet closed within my heart. There has to be more than this! If I tell my story, maybe, just maybe, I will get out of this cage and fly far, far away toward my true reflection and be able to express who I am!"

Chapter 27

Father, Father, Father

"A person's safest place
is the family — a small
crack can destroy your
whole life."

– Black Money Love

Father, Father, Father

I saw it all
you
You,
chose not

I chose to heal
me
Me,
I choose

I took the fall
hard
Hard,
not to

I left your path
turned
Turned,
faced me

You could not face
truth
Truth,
be told

Her Story

Father, Father, Father

She looks at her reflection in the mirror. She sees a face stained with pain but also a survivor who lives with wisdom on her side. She chooses to stand tall in triumph — unashamed. For most of her life, she was haunted and handled by perpetrators. But the cycle is done. She grieves what she knows and takes responsibility to protect herself.

But more importantly, she is awakened to the truth about her father: silence does not bring truth. Silence is a slow killer of *self*. On the other hand, voicing the truth is the most powerful and transformational instrument in the world, even when the revelation of *what is* felt painful and is difficult to process.

Does she forgive him? Yes. Even considering his lack of admittance. Does she wish upon him freedom? Of course. But not forgetting is the key to keeping the jewels in her treasure chest so she can protect her heart and never again be disillusioned. She stops trying to rescue him, to protect herself, the unhealthy pattern she had been following — save the man, lose herself, and repeat the cycle. They were both terrified of the truth. But she alone, decided to acknowledge the gospel and let go of the sins of the father. Her decision has set them free.

Her soul remembers the impact. Her spirit sees the truth. Grace is freedom.

Listen to the Music

"Now We Are Free / Honor Him," by Hans Zimmer,
performed by Jacob Ladegaard

Chapter 28

The Gift

Sincerity of heart is
true love wrapped up in
a gift.

The Gift

I have a gift for you
It is meant to be cherished
It has value and worth

Sentiment

Will you accept it
Or reject it?
Protect it
Or damage it?

Sentiment

Will you open it
Or forget it?
Untie it
Or cage it?

Sentiment

For what is in a gift
But a key to unlock
The heart's path of passion

Sentiment

Meet it
Greet it
Feel it
Reach for it

Her Story

The Gift

So many men, so little time. So many lifetimes expressed in this one moment in time! She asks, "For what reason?" Sentiment can be taken from these circumstances — the sentiment of suffering and the sentiment of triumph. Sentiment embodies the deepest meaning of human consciousness and expression. It is meant to be cherished. It holds all the emotions of the heart, such as tenderness, sadness, and elation. It is filled with infinite value and worth. Sentiment adds life to life itself. It does not subtract from the equation, leaving a balance of zero. No.

She has a choice to accept the gift of sentiment within the nucleus of her hands and stroke it with awe and tender care. Or she can reject it, leaving herself bare and broken, holding a dearth of emotional wealth. She can also protect it by embracing how it reveals itself in its purest form. Or damage it by ignoring its intrinsic purpose. The soul holds the impact surrounding the incarnation and resurrection of the spirit within the human experience.

The key is to live this experience from the beginning until the end with desire and passion, for eventually, freedom will lead her on the right path, but if the sentiment of *living* is forgotten or caged, freedom will not be found, and the imprisoning of goodness and humility will be locked up forever. The key to her heart's path of passion is meeting, greeting, feeling, and reaching toward the sentiment of her heart, encompassing and honouring all of her experiences. Walking this path will empower her to embrace ALL of what the Universe has spun her way. Like a whirlwind confronted, her sincerity of heart takes control of a beautiful life awaiting her arrival, hiding no expression of her true identity. She becomes the wind to her wheels, spinning in the direction of great inner power and a glorious awakening!

Listen to the Music

"I Say a Little Prayer," by Aretha Franklin

Chapter 29

Wind in My Wheels

Life is like a storm. She blew in, caught her wind, and breathed out transformation. Be the storm, the force of nature that brings about the wind of change!

Wind in My Wheels

Wind in my wheels
Blow me home
To a place
I call my own

Where I may see
Her inner works
Where life goes on
Her precious quirks

Bit fingernails
Red lips aglow
Blue eyes that pierce
Kinky hair a-flow

Voice that sings
Mouth to kiss
A crate of care
Heartsight of bliss

Wandering mind
Spokes of steel
Strength, you feel
Spirited, real

Wind in my wheels
Blow me home
To a place
I call my own

Her Story

Wind in My Wheels

She is ready to brave the storm. The wind of change has become her friend. The wind is her strength. She is becoming victorious, joyful, and ever so connected with the Divine. She is love. She captivates all of humanity with her beauty, drawing near to those who need her salutations.

Firmly around her neck, she secures the mystery of multiple revelations. She is ready to fully unite with the home inside her heart, the one that was lost constellations ago but is now found in the world of the present.

"Wind in my wheels, blow me home, to a place I call my own." Her eyes, once black holes that swallowed all the light, have become the windows to her soul, and she is filled with galaxies of stars. Others are drawn towards her glow and filled with warmth in the presence of her light force. Finally, she's free to shine as bright as a neutron star!

She accepts her quirky, unique nature, no longer inviting the shunning and sabotaging effects previously endured. Ultimately, she enjoys the fruit of her perseverance; her raw-bitten fingernails reveal courage during times of trials, her red lips aglow divulge her ability to ensnare, her blue eyes pierce the burning truth from a psychic flame, and her kinky blonde hair twirls and bounces as she squeals with innocent delight!

She has a voice, and she's going to use it, a mouth to kiss dear tears away, a crate of care to hold you with, and a heart of bliss to dream upon. Her wandering mind and vivid imagination bring life to miracles, still time. Her spokes of steel and the wind in her wheels spin with strength and inner determination.

She carries with her the spirit of a girl, so real, so alive, so playful and free! She doesn't need to hide beneath the sins of others anymore. The wind of change has arrived, and she is ready.

Listen to the Music

"Colors of the Wind," by Tori Kelly

Chapter 30

God Hid an Engine in Me

Drive towards a destiny of freedom, not confinement.

God Hid an Engine in Me

The face of majesty
Why are you mucho
far from me?
I look to find
but do not see
Where God could truly be

I search on road, farther
for Higher Wisdom
I must see!
Yet, look inside
front, back, both sides
until a *hum* goes by

An Engine's voice speaks up
"Fill tank, your fuel's
gone empty!"
Those miles, apart
when here, are plenty
Drive! Not slow, go Venti!

A Hellcat of an engine
Tailor-made, revved up
like a deuce
to floor, footloose
skid marks, pursuit
the breaking of a noose

Steer clear of character
defamation, in the box
four-way stop
Look left, look right
rear mirror, signs *pop*
Take back the road on top

HOLY HOT ROD HORSE STRENGTH!
Such power is not far
under hood
Inside you *rumble*
"*Our* oil is good!"
Now, God is understood

Her Story

God Hid an Engine in Me

She has found and identified her wheel of destiny. It was inside her all along. The God of her understanding, the one who is not confined to the inside of a box, put a powerful engine in her so she could move through her pain amid lessons learned and drive toward a destiny filled with freedom. She thought God was far away, a distant voice muffled by silence. But in reality, she had built a wall around herself to hide from the terror of pain. She hid because she was scared and wounded.

Her search for a higher power has been relentless! Yet, in her mind, she kept travelling to faraway destinations that lacked provision for her future. When exhausted attempts are not matched with relief, she is forced to look within — the answers have been inside of her all along. Here, she hears a loud rumble. The hum of an engine, the God inside of her speaks up!

"Fill your tank; your fuel has gone empty!"

Miles apart from her identity and searching outside of herself for answers has left her burning unnecessary fuel with little result. But God put an engine in her! And not just any old engine, a Hellcat made to move! It's time she accelerates to her destination. She slides into the seat of her newest destination and turns the key toward her destiny. She's revved up like a deuce! By pressing the pedal to the floor, she activates the powerful connection between her and the engine, the strength underneath her very own foot. She is no longer tied to one location. She is finally footloose and free from confinement! She drives like there are no limits, making her mark along the way. She is empowered to pursue the breaking of a noose, the rope that once hung tightened around her neck, silencing her inner character.

She no longer allows defaming characters to steal her identity or ill-centred mindsets to trap her in a box, like a four-way stop. She gives heed to the signs that appear in the rearview mirror, lessons from the past, so she can take back the road ahead of her. Horsepower strength is not far from reach because her pursuit of freedom is better understood. The rumble inside of her is her Higher Power, the oil of lubrication, giving her the ability to put the pedal to the metal and make things happen!

She's been given an engine, a god-like power that connects her to a source that represents *her reflection of truth.* She is on a road worth travelling.

Listen to the Music

"Black Betty," performed by Ram Jam

Chapter 31

The Garden of Silk

A road travelled has turns, curves, rubble, and roadblocks; however, the path of lessons learned is as smooth as silk, when understood.

The Garden of Silk

Master of the Garden of Silk
Fortress, where floral rose and citrus grows
Green earth besieges, starvation halts
Immersion flows, pressed oil seeps

Oh, wall of love
Defend me, dear
From merchant jewels and ancient trade
To make believe true love as this?

No! In its place, adorn inside
A heart of gold to stroke me with
And suck with mouth a breast that soothes
Lips to swallow, folds of dew

Almond tip to bite for pleasure
Statue trunk, mid-thigh, such length!
Reach her canal, must tremble deep
Enter slowly, as emotion seeps

Push hard to see the lioness!
She will surrender bliss to thee
On hands and knees, earth warms her chest
The Master's Garden to her He bequeaths

Her Story

The Garden of Silk

Down on her knees, not in tears but in humble awe of what existed inside of her all along, she lays down her life in the Garden of Silk, where worms give birth to soft threads of white tulle that caress her naked body. Scents of floral rose and citrus fruit awaken her to a Persian Eden. Crossing the navel of the earth, four elements join together — sky, earth, water, and vegetation — bringing her boundless life.

Under her living body, where she lay with outstretched arms on green earth so ripe for planting, olives seep a lubricous oil, saturating her body with an anointment of protection. The Master has designed a sanctuary, a walled fortress of love for her, to keep evil out. The great wall defends her from intruders, and she is kept safe. It is solid in construction, spreading itself far and wide, running for thousands of miles to protect her from imitation love: those who see wealth as a way to live yet have little regard for the *Spirit of Love* and ancient rituals that trade a woman's spirit for the devil's pleasure.

Touched with the character of love, she is immersed in great power! She declares that she will never again settle for the deceit of destruction to take hold of her life. "NO!" Her desire to partner with true intimacy begins with a request from the Master of the Garden of Silk.

"In compensation for what I've been through, grant me a heart of gold." She asks for all bitterness, resentment, and hatred to leave her, giving her breasts that soothe and nurture the frailty out of humanity. And lips that speak wisdom into the hearts of those who are ignorant, leaving a dew of light to awaken sleeping souls.

She asks for an exchange of bliss and pleasure instead of abuse and trauma. A monument — a statue, endowed with great size, to remind her of how the pain has penetrated her and yet, the immense joy found in freedom has released and disintegrated sustained suffering. An intimate love-making rhythm is channelled throughout her body and forces out intense emotions that had been buried coffin-deep.

She's ready to release her lioness! Her eyes are open. She sees and surrenders to her inner power. With gratitude, on hands and knees, she bows down to the Master who has created the earth out of love and adoration for her. In a Persian Eden, a garden of protection, she is illuminated in a cloak of tulle, crafted of white spun silk, and is now recognized as *a spirit of light.*

Listen to the Music

"Night in a Persian Garden," performed by Time Machine

Chapter 32

Cracked Glass

Beauty is restored when
what becomes lost is sent
away to be found.

Cracked Glass

Cracked glass
Shattered faces
Bloodstained linen
Blowing in the wind

Cracked glass
Shattered faces
Broke me into pieces
Pick me up again

Sharp lip
Double-edged sword
Force of nature
Try to be my friend

Cutthroat
Freedom granted
Mouth wide open
Hear my voice, to mend

Tears flow
No more sorrow
Come, tomorrow
Love, a heart will send

Cracked glass
Shattered faces
Glue together
Fly with me again

Cracked glass
Show my face
Pure white linen
Blowing in the wind

I looked
In broken mirror
Now you, can too
We can be akin

Her Story

Cracked Glass

Even though dark forces sought to extinguish her inner fire and smother her from the breath of life itself, she unceasingly pursued the spirit of light that now surrounds her illuminated and enlightened soul. In the same way, a glass mirror cracks when struck by a force stronger than itself; particles of darkness shatter when touched by a light force. Darkness disappears and burns to ashes when surrounded in an atmosphere ruled by the intimate bond between light and love.

For most of her life, she looked through cracked glass and saw a distorted reflection of herself. The long-term effect of abuse and brainwashing had ripped to shreds her pure heart, an image represented as blood-stained linen blowing in the wind. She doubted and saw her whole self as *ugly*. But now, after grieving what was lost and certainly aware of what has been found, she finds consolation in the words of the Mystic Rumi: "The wound is the place where the light enters you."

Dark forces once penetrated her voice, silencing the symbol, her mouth, designed to tell the truth and stop the perpetuation of dishonesty. Even though a sword of lies stabbed at her jugular, her throat, trying to sever all ties to her inner power, she arose and became known. Remembering and reflecting became a reminder to never again partner with anything or anyone who tries to steal her strength, potential, and identity. Freedom is to live with a mouth wide open; hence, the voice of true identity can be expressed, while at the same time, having the ability to mend wounds and heal great sorrow.

An emotional wound heals with love. It then transforms into a sacred scar. Pain that once pricked the soul with slivers, leaving fibres torn and layers wounded, becomes Higher Wisdom, strength of mind, and power that penetrates. It's not just ordinary love that fabricates healing. It is the art of compassionate affection that mends inescapable suffering and caresses tears with tender endearment. Compassion turns misery into a bright, shining star that leads the way through darkness and affliction and fondles a bleeding heart with care as it is held in an open hand, carrying the weight of trauma. Heart strokes of sincerity create emotional wounds to heal, sacred scars to be noticed, and lead souls to freedom: a form of art, in the name of love.

As she connects to her pain within the mind of a woman, no longer a child, she's able to move away from denial. She acknowledges her grief and loss as a part of life. Simultaneously, the light of love and its translucent glow of truth glue together broken pieces of her fractured existence. The shattered faces, the sins of others who painted her as the villain in response to their avoidance of self-accountability, in the end, ignite in her a passion, an intimate pursuit to connect with the essence and core character of her youth. This newly bonded relationship sets her free to see herself as loved, not defective, disgraced, or impure. She is now like pure white linen blowing in the wind — shameless, and blemish-free.

"When I look in the mirror, I see the truth, and I reflect on the words once given to me in the spirit of love."

If you saw what I saw, you would love yourself more.
If you see what I see, you will accept yourself the way I do.

As if being spoken to by love in its purest form, she takes one last look in the mirror and remembers who she truly is, beyond the bruises, the blood-stained tears, the mascara-filled eyes, and the makeup-smudged face. She is a woman worthy of love. She not only captured her demons; she hunted them down, turned them loose, and laid them to rest at the foot and face of the Character of Love.

When times were unbearable and she felt there was no other choice but to give up, a voice inside her said, "You only wanted to go this far, but I'm taking you all the way!" And that is exactly what she did. "Screw second base, I'm going for a home run!"

She found the key to the treasure chest, her heart — the spirit of a girl who can open doors, unleash the power to remove darkness and fulfill a destiny designed to express her innate worth and value as a woman. The faces of those who had painted her with their chains of imprisonment and excluded her from the table of life no longer have the ability to mark her with shame. She is free to fulfill her holy grail. She has learned to trust her instincts, designed to protect her from harm. She reclaims her voice so as not to betray it again. She trusts her awareness even when it aggravates another's façade. Loneliness and isolation became a contemplative place where she could look at the truth, and transform. She has transformed tragedy, abuse, betrayal and abandonment into a triumphant journey — for herself and others. *She* is a gift.

A girl with a dream must not die, but to the death, she was spared; dare to dream. She does not live with the dread of despair inside of her, with dreams unfulfilled, but embraces her true nature, love, in partnership with the *Sacred Heart of Truth*.

She looked in the mirror, saw her reflection, arose, and became known. She found the seed of her youth, her true identity, the spirit of a girl — the answers, the truth.

And the spirit of the wolf? He is the young man from the alleyway who laid down his life for her, to guide her toward *Higher Wisdom* and teach her how to discern character. If any God there may be, it is the *Divine Character of Love*, a contemplative, meaningful connection and communion with creation and compassion itself. This interconnection personifies the comfort found when discovering the sacred amid the mystery of the unknown — the dualism between light and darkness.

Listen to the Music

"The First Time Ever I Saw Your Face," by Roberta Flack

I have wept a willow of a weeping tree. I can now smile as the tears drop away. And so can you.

Never end a story without a song.

Listen to the Music

"A Sky Full of Stars," by Coldplay

Turn this song up LOUD and DANCE!

Until We Meet Again…

ACKNOWLEDGMENTS

I am thankful for my children. My son, you are the light of my life. As I watched you grow, I learned much from you: to enjoy life, embrace simple pleasures, and create joy. You are a gift to me. My daughter, I love you more than you could ever know. I would also like to acknowledge her for the artwork on the cover of this book.

I am grateful for my ever-so-available mentor, Rhonda. Without your patience, wisdom grace and listening ear, where would I be? It is true. Mentors can be the best teachers, healers and guides.

To my father, with deep pain and grace. To my mother, with deep understanding and forgiveness.

Looking back, I remember my grade two teacher, Miss Martin. Her sincerity touched my heart. She made words come alive on the chalkboard! This brought me true happiness and ignited a spark to write forever.

My affection reaches out to the one man who awakened me to my worth and value. Your love changed my life. You know who you are — the one who sketched me a picture of a dragonfly and bought me my favourite painting, *The Kiss*.

With sincere appreciation, I would like to recognize Dania Sheldon, who holds a doctorate in English Language and Literature from the University of Oxford, for her contribution to editing.

And last, but not least, to Carmen. You are my Angel on the other side. Even though your spirit rests in peace, I know you are here, to guide me along the way and share the tale of wisdom — my forever love and guide, The Wolf.

ABOUT THE AUTHOR

(That's Me)

Victoria is a lover of words, song, and soul, the very language that inspires her to turn the mind into a bleeding, open heart. She is a lyrical songwriter known for musical notes that jump onto her lap and land on her fingertips. Behind her smile, she is a mystery — deep waters brewing under the surface. As a Mystic Visionary, she connects the dots to the Sacred Heart of Truth, bringing love messages from the Divine, Angels, Spirit Guides, and Helpers on the other side. Her *Art of Intuitive and Compassionate Listening* teaches individuals to connect with their true identity and to love their story, even when it hurts. She encourages the journey towards Higher Wisdom, the place where intuition, heart-sight, and clear-seeing defy logic — the path towards freedom. She holds a Bachelor of Arts degree in Sociology, Psychology, and is certified in Spiritual Care.

Victoria Starr Love's Contact

https://www.victoriastarrlove.com

VOICE YOUR TRUTH

My voice is worth hearing. What I have to say is valuable and important. My experiences count. I am worthy of security, stability, good health, and prosperity. I can do whatever I want to accomplish. My me makes millions; I am rich in heart, wealthy in spirit, and financially powerful for the common good of all people. Success follows me wherever I go. My fingerprint to success is knowing, believing, and walking out my true identity without a shadow of a doubt. This can be Your Fingerprint to Success, too.

www.ingramcontent.com/pod-product-compliance
Lightning Source LLC
Chambersburg PA
CBHW032052020426
42335CB00011B/301